RIPPING CLOUDS: THE TRUTH ABOUT VAPING

By
Kimo Kiyabu

Copyright © 2016 Kimo Kiyabu

All rights reserved.

ISBN-10:1522914935
ISBN-13:978-1522914938
Kimokiyabu@rocketmail.com

This is dedicated to those who seek the truth.

THE JOURNEY BEGINS...

It was October in 2012. I had just started attending Le Cordon Bleu College of Culinary Arts in Las Vegas, Nevada. I was smoking a pack-a-day when the subject of smoking and cooking came up.

Smoking is frowned upon greatly in the culinary world. When a chef smokes a few things are affected. When you cook you have to use your sense of smell, sight, and taste. Most importantly, the sense of smell, and taste. Scientific research has found that smoking dulls a person taste buds. In culinary school you are trained to constantly taste the food your cooking to see if the product needs more seasoning. If your palate is dull, then you may over season, or under season what you are cooking. If you have ever gone out to a restaurant and have consumed food that tasted like it has more salt than the ocean—then you'll know what I'm talking about.

Also when a person smokes they often smell like an ashtray. But when your the smoker, you don't really notice it. In school they do not allow students to wear cologne or perfume because the smell effects how you smell your food. So when your a smoker your smell may effect not only your smell, but when those around you who are also trying to smell what they are cooking. I have only recently noticed this effect in the past few years after quitting.

I remember one instance when I was trying to determine if the bag of herbs I had in my hands was either Italian Parsley or Cilantro. Both herbs look similar, small green leafs with stems, however, Cilantro has a very distinct smell. When I tried to smell the difference between the two, I could only smell the effects of the cigarette on my co-worker, who was standing next to me. I had to leave the walk-in refrigerator to determine which one was Cilantro.

This career change I had started, put the seed in my head, that I needed to quit smoking. I had already tried to quit with the nicotine patch. I had also tried the gum and the prescription pills. Always, after a week or so, I would go back to smoking. I had lasted the longest, one month, with the E-cigarette. But the taste was horrible and always left a metallic after taste.

While going to culinary school I had continued to work as a city bus driver. I used to drive the double-decker buses on the strip. One day I had seen another bus driver with this strange device around her neck. I have since forgot the woman's name but she had explained that the device was a vaporizer. The device looked similar to a writing pen, with a tank, and a mouth piece. I watched as she demonstrated and I was intrigued.

I saved up the hundred dollars and purchased this new device. To say it was comparable to smoking was arguable. But I had to try and stay disciplined. After all I was tired of smoking. I had become fed up with having to go outside, in the cold winter months, if I wanted to have a cigarette. I was tired of constantly being told I smelled like an ashtray by everyone. I was spending a fortune on body sprays that I would use to try to cover the scent of the cigarette. I was annoyed with having to go to an authorized smoke area to have my cancer stick. Not to mention the smoking rooms at the airport was absolutely ridiculous.

So I was determined to stick with the vaporizer even though it didn't feel like a great substitute for smoking at the time. To make things worse this was about the time that non smokers began bad mouthing the E-cigarettes and vaporizers. But my fellow students took notice of my vaporizer and a trend started after I began vaping. I would notice every week one or two more students going out and trying the vaporizer for themselves. Soon I became an activist for vaping at my school.

The rumors, bad-mouthing, and myths concerning vaping continued to get worse in the months to come. I found myself getting pissed at the anti-vaping society. Here I finally found a way to get my nicotine fix that didn't smell bad or affected anyone around me. But here they were saying it was just as bad as smoking. That vaporizers should fall under the clean air act and fall under the cigarette bans.

I remember watching news reports from Chicago and New York when they were putting bans on vaporizers. They showed a New York courtroom and people, attending the hearing, started chanting, "Vaping isn't smoking!"

I remember becoming a protester, walking down the hallways of my school, vaping. Going to Disneyland, walking around the park, vaping blatantly. To my disbelief, both my school, and Disneyland gave me the same exact statement. "Sir, we know your not smoking, but it's the *act of*. It simulates the act of smoking."

"What!? Are you f—king kidding me?" Well I didn't cuss because cussing in Disneyland is just as bad as cussing in a church. Needless to say I was furious concerning the boneheaded thought process.

A month or so later I had been given an assignment from my English teacher. Our class had to do a research paper backed by scientific research. We had to use case studies that had been published. In class we were taught how to research, finding case studies on our subject, and how to properly write the citations. It hit me immediately…I would research vaping. Little did I know at the time, but this assignment would put me on a path. I would try to conquer the world's fear about vaping through knowledge. This began my journey into the truth about vaping.

HISTORY OF THE VAPORIZER

When it comes to vaping, history plays a crucial part in preventing foolish laws, restricting the use of vaporizers. The number one reason being fear. People fear what they do not know or understand. Unfortunately that is the case in this situation. People fear vaping because they do not really understand vaping.

To understand vaping we must first look at the electronic cigarette. Many have come to believe that the electronic cigarette was first invented in 2003 by a 52 year-old pharmacist named Hon Lik in Beijing, China. Contrary to popular belief this is simply not true.

The first electronic cigarette was patented 53 years ago by Herbert Gilbert in 1963. His attempt to produce and sell on the mass market failed, causing his invention to be forgotten.

Then in 1988 the R.J. Reynolds Tobacco Company attempted their own version of the electronic cigarette called *Premier* cigarettes. The first users of the product complained so much about how bad the taste was, it never gained popularity. The Premier cigarette was taken off the market, less than a year after it's release, in 1989. In 1994 R.J. Reynolds tried once again renaming the cigarette to *Eclipse*. The name change did not effect the outcome. Once again smokers complained and the Eclipse failed to satisfy.

Then in 2003 Hon Lik, who may have not invented the first electronic cigarette, did in fact, perfect it.

Just like the electronic cigarette, the vaporizer is far from new technology. In fact, the first vaporizer dates back 134 years ago! As you can see in the following pages, these ads ran in the local paper, in San Francisco, from 1882 to the early 1900's.

INVINCIBLE!
—THE—
Carbolic Smoke Ball
(TRADE MARK.)

FREE TESTS!   **FREE TESTS!**

NEVER FAILS TO CURE

Catarrh, Asthma, Diphtheria, Croup, Neuralgia, Hay Fever, Bronchitis, Cold in the Head, Sore Throat, Etc.

SHOULD BE IN EVERY HOUSEHOLD.

A CHILD CAN USE IT.

Not Sold by Druggists

Circulars, Testimonials, Etc., Sent to any Address Free.

Genuine Home Testimonials can be seen at our office.

SENT, ON RECEIPT OF PRICE, TO ANY PART OF THE WORLD.

MAIL ORDERS. "Smoke Ball" and "Debellator" packages sent by mail, with full directions, on receipt of price, $5.00 (Smoke Ball, $3.00; Debellator, $2.00), two 2-cent stamps. Remit by Postal Note, Wells, Fargo & Co., or Postoffice Money Order, Registered Letter, or in coin by express.

CARBOLIC SMOKE BALL CO.,

Rooms 7, 8, 9, 10, No. 652 Market St., Cor. Kearny (opp. Lotta Fountain), San Francisco, Cal.
☛ Separate Parlor for Ladies, who will be waited upon by skilled and polite lady attendants.

WILSON'S VAPORIZING INHALER!
A Household Treasure.

MEDICATED INHALATIONS.

The only successful home treatment for CATARRH, ASTHMA, BRONCHITIS, Colds, Throat and Lung troubles, etc. Come and see us. Trial free. Hundreds of recorded cures in this city. Price, complete with medicine, only $2.50. Sent by express anywhere. Satisfaction guaranteed. Cure yourself. No fees to pay. Office, 229 Kearny street, San Francisco.

***

The first actual patent for the electric vaporizer was filed May 3rd, 1923 by Harold Wilson. Which has been the basis for all other electric vaporizers since then.

The basis for the vaporizer is simple. A heating source heats a liquid creating a vapor that is then inhaled by a person. Since 1882 the sole purpose of the vaporizer has been for medical purposes. You will soon see nothing has change, even today.

For anyone to fear the vaporizer by using the statement, "It's new, so they don't know how it will effect the human body in ten or twenty years," is absurd since the technology has been around 93 years. It's obvious in 2016 that people lack the knowledge to understand or realize what the vaporizer actually is.

Many people remember as a child, having a cold, and their guardian using a vaporizer to break up congestion in their chest. Before they turned on the vaporizer they would pour a liquid into the water. That liquid was Vick's VapoSteam and parents have been using it since 1963. Yes, for fifty-three years, vaporizers using VapoSteam, has helped children during the cold season.

So it's surprising that nobody has realized that the vaporizer, used to help people quit smoking, is the exact same thing. Those people I had seen in the New York courtroom, chanting, "vaping isn't smoking," they were absolutely correct. It's time for the world to stop ignoring the history. It's the history, that provides the proof, concerning the effects of vaping on the human body.

PROPYLENE GLYCOL, VEGETABLE GLYCERIN, AND NICOTINE...ARE THEY REALLY EVIL?

I remember one day I had been putting a build onto my Box Mod at my computer desk. Just as my wife walked in, I triggered the Mod to see if the wire coils were lighting correctly, before putting in the cotton. Next thing I heard was, "oh my god, why is it doing that? Is that safe?" Her reaction to the coils lighting and becoming bright red got me thinking. For people who don't vape; watching a person vape might be kind of mind boggling. Like when tribesman or Native Americans first seen the rifle. They were not sure of what to make of it. Calling the rifle such names as boom stick, thunder stick, or "magic stick that go boom."

So for those readers who currently do not vape, I will explain how the vaporizer or, "the magic box that goes sizzle," works.

First there is a Mechanical Mod or a Box Mod. Mod coming from the word *Modification*. Before there were these elaborate "Mods" people would modify flashlights and turn them into vaporizers. The Mod provides the power, from batteries, to heat wire coils in the Atomizer.

The Atomizer, sometimes called *Atty* for short, is a metal housing that screws into the Mod. Inside the Atomizer are connection points for wire coils to attach to. The wire coils, not only help to complete the wire circuit, they also heat up, as the circuit is completed. Cotton is placed inside the coil similar to threading a needle. The cotton and coil become soaked with the vaping liquid. Then the final part of the electrical circuit is completed by depressing a trigger mechanism and allowing the electrical current from the battery to flow through the circuit. When the electric current reaches the wire coils; the coils heat up to a minimum of 370° Fahrenheit. Thus turning the liquid into a vapor. Still having trouble comprehending? No problem. Imagine an electric stove. Turn on the electric stove to high, see how the stove gets red hot? Now take a roll of paper towels, soak the roll in water, now put the wet roll of paper towels on the red hot stove. See the steam rising up? That's vapor.

There's no magic to it really. In a home vaporizer, where Vick's VapoSteam is poured into, the heating coil is the center piece that the electric cord is connected to. The water mixed with the VapoSteam liquid, is in essence, the same as vaping liquid.

All the working mechanical parts of the vaporizer has never really been the problem. The worry and fear has always been due to what's in the vapor. To understand this better; we must take a closer look at the liquid.

I had been vaping for about a year when I walked into a vapor store and the salesman was trying to convince me why I should buy his particular brand of vaping liquid. As he was prepping a tester for me to try their version of Fruit Loops flavored liquid, he tells me, "Yeah our juice is all natural, the other guys use glycol we only use PG and VG." Trying not to be a total asshole, I just smiled and thought to myself, "What in the hell." Now understand, I had already completed my research on the vaporizer, and I expected that someone working in a vape shop should know more than what I knew. A couple of years later I was in yet another vape shop, sitting at the tasting bar, talking to the clerk when a lady comes in, pushing a baby stroller. She makes her way through the clouds, purchases her liquid, then leaves. The clerk then states, "I know vaping is better than smoking, but I wouldn't expose my child to it."

It's this type of thinking and statements that really prompted me to write this book concerning vaping. I understand people who do not vape or smokers who try to stand up for their habit, as in the case of my niece. But for people in the industry, there is no excuse for them to be ignorant or speak with ignorance.

The juice, the liquid, however you want to call it. It is the reason people fear the vaporizer. In this chapter I will break it down in hopes to educate the masses. Now before I get started I will remind you, the reader, this is not a research paper. I will not be placing citations throughout the pages. However, I will include, at the end of this book, where you can find all the research that I have mentioned in this book. Now with that being said—"on to the liquid!"

Juice—Liquid—eJuice—eLiquid—eLixir—eNectar—eSauce—your mamma's E, no matter what you may call it, this is the liquid, that turns into vapor, that you inhale into your lungs. It is composed of five ingredients at the very maximum. First it may contain water. Do I really need to describe H2O? I didn't think so. Next is Propylene Glycol, then Vegetable Glycerin, Nicotine, and finally flavoring.

I was at culinary school a little over a month when a fellow student notice my new vaporizer, as I puffed it, while hanging out with the smoking students in my class. Let's call her Angela(name changed). Angela came up and said, "Is that one of those vapor pens?"

"Yeah, why?" I responded.

"You know your smoking anti-freeze, right?" She said.

"What are you talking about?"

"The liquid. It's the stuff they put into anti-freeze."

That night I watched my local news channel and seen where Angela had received her information from. The news station reported that an ingredient in the vaping pen liquid was a main component to anti-freeze. The ingredient being Propylene Glycol.

While doing my research I found out that there are actually two types of Propylene Glycol. Yes the first type is a main component in anti-freeze. However, I noticed a slight difference on the ingredient list for my vaping liquid. The liquid listed Propylene Glycol USP. Then I asked myself, "what exactly is USP?"

USP stands for United States Pharmacopeial Convention. They are a scientific nonprofit organization that was founded in 1820. They set the standards for what is safe for human consumption worldwide. They not only identify. They test for strength, quality, and purity of medicines, food ingredients, and dietary supplements manufactured, distributed and consumed worldwide. So when you see the USP logo, then you know it is safe for human consumption. Obviously, the news source had not been due diligent in researching their story. But it doesn't end there.

In February 1945 a report that was published in the American Journal of Medical Sciences told how a test was conducted that showed the effects of Propylene Glycol on children. The test was done over a three year period from 1941 to 1944. They conducted the test at a seaside children's hospital. The children, who were confined to their beds due to illness, were split up into two different wings. One wing was exposed to Propylene Glycol vapor for three years. The other wing had just their normal conditions. The children's wing that had normal conditions experienced 132 cases of respiratory infections. Over the same three year period, the wing that had been treated with Propylene Glycol vapor, only had 13 cases of respiratory infections! Propylene Glycol had been very effective in preventing respiratory infections. The scientists were able to determine that the Propylene Glycol actually killed the airborne bacteria in the wing.

I guess this is why when I had been smoking, I would get a chest cold every year around Thanksgiving. Since I have been vaping…I have not had a chest cold yet. So I have no problem vaping around my seven year-old son whether it be in the car or the house. And if your wondering, the answer is no, he has never had a respiratory infection.

But wait! There's more. In 2006 the Environmental Protection Agency tested Propylene Glycol as an inhalant. They found that Propylene Glycol had no toxins or carcinogens and found that it was safe for humans to inhale. Which was not surprising since 62 years prior to their findings they had already tested it on kids.

So from this we can conclude that Propylene Glycol or PG will not cause any health issues and is not evil. If anything, the more people using Personal Vaporizers in the world, will mean less respiratory infections in the world, and cleaner air. So if your vaping and someone scoffs. Tell them, "your welcome. Because of me; you probably won't get a respiratory infection. My Propylene Glycol is cleaning the air and fighting pollution!"

The next ingredient, Vegetable Glycerin or VG, is a clear, odorless liquid produced from plant oils, typically palm oil, soy, or coconut oil. Vegetable Glycerin can be found in many foods like, cheese, yogurt, breads, and many beverages as well. Vegetable Glycerin can be also found in many medications, cosmetics, and products for infants. It is not only edible it is also safe to inhale. Vegetable Glycerin is often a replacement for alcohol. It has been approved by the Federal Food and Drug Administration. Along with the Environmental Protection Agency and the United States Pharmacopeial Convention. So again, VG is not evil. Leaving the last ingredient to look at…Nicotine.

In 2007 I worked as a pool bartender at Bellagio Hotel and Casino in Las Vegas. Erected in different sections around the pool area stood tent-like structures called cabanas. In the cabana you'll find a breakfast table, dressing area, sink, refrigerator, flat screen television, and daybeds. Basically a small hotel room near the pool. The cabana can be closed giving the occupants absolute privacy.

One morning I had been told that a V.I.P. wanted a

bartender to go to his cabana and show him how to make a berry mojito. Our berry mojito at the time had been a big hit and the presentation was simply beautiful. To make the berry mojito we would muddle lime, mint, simple syrup, blueberries, raspberries, and strawberries. Then added rum, ice, and topped it with soda. After stirring the concoction, a garnish of mint, a strawberry, a blueberry, and a raspberry would be set on top. Finally a tap of powdered sugar on top of the berries.

Yes, it took a minute to create one of these drinks, and I had been elected to show our very important person the how-tos.

I gathered what I had needed from the bar and made my way to the V.I.P. cabana. I entered the cabana and had been caught off guard to find a very famous actor, that I will leave nameless, sitting on a chair smoking a cigarette. It had been known that this actor had been diagnosed with Parkinson's Disease. What I didn't know is that he smoked cigarettes.

I introduced myself ignoring the fact he was smoking and I acted like he was just another typical guest. I began my presentation answering his questions as I made the drink. I noticed that he not only smoked, but that he was a chain smoker. I myself was a smoker at the time and the smoke started to bother me. I couldn't help myself. I just had to ask, "Sir, I didn't know you smoked."

"Oh, I'm sorry, is it bothering you?"

"No, I smoke to. I just never heard of you smoking."

"I know. I try to keep it from the public. I smoke, it helps with my Parkinson's and the shaking."

"Really?" I said, probably with a look of disbelief.

"Yeah doctors think that nicotine can help make it a

little more bearable."

That is the first time I had heard about the effects of nicotine and how it could help with those with Parkinson's. Scientists also thought that nicotine could prevent Parkinson's.

This thinking also had been the basis for a scientific research article published in the magazine Annals of Neurology titled, *Nicotine from edible Solanaceae and risk of Parkinson disease*. In this article that had been written by five doctors who concluded that people who consume tomatoes, potatoes, eggplants, and any type of pepper. Whether they know it or not are consuming nicotine. Ever wonder why you like french fries so much? Maybe because it has nicotine. That's right, your love of pizza or spicy food might be the cause of nicotine.

And it doesn't matter if it's a Bell pepper or a Jalapeño pepper…they all contain nicotine. Yes the world has been consuming nicotine all this time—and didn't even know it.

So the biggest marketer of nicotine to kids might be McDonald's and their happy meal that contains both tomatoes and potatoes.

But let's not get out of hand here. Make no mistake, the liquid nicotine that is contained in vaping liquid, though maybe helpful in preventing Parkinson's, is still very dangerous to children.

So if your reading this, thinking you want to make your own vaping liquid, that's great. You may need to buy the liquid nicotine in bulk. Sold in liter bottles or larger. Please…no let me say this again…PLEASE PLEASE PLEASE…DON'T BE STUPID! ESPECIALLY IF YOU HAVE KIDS! KEEP THE NICOTINE UNDER LOCK AND KEY! ACT IF AS THOUGH YOU ARE

HANDLING A BOMB OR GUN. THE LIQUID NICOTINE THAT IS USED IN VAPING LIQUID WILL KILL YOUR KIDS!

This industry doesn't need some idiot killing kids because they do not know what they are doing as they try to mix their own liquid. If the nicotine splashes or spills on an adult, they'll probably become very sick. If it splashes or spills on a child...THEY COULD DIE! Got it. Good.

Just like anything else, too much of something can cause adverse side effects. A person can overdose on vitamin A, B-12, or other healthy products. It doesn't mean something is bad for you, it just means you over did it. Same with nicotine. If you want to see what this is like, do the following. Get a drip atomizer, then drip onto the cotton 24mg nicotine vaping liquid. Now take ten big puffs one right after another. What you feel next will feel a little like motion sickness. This is called being *"Nic Sick."* It's when you have overdosed on nicotine. However, this does not prove Nicotine is necessarily evil. What we do know is that Nicotine is an addictive, natural, stimulant that is found in peppers, tomatoes, eggplants, and potatoes. Nicotine may prevent Parkinson's and could reduce the effects of Parkinson's. Nicotine is a performance-enhancing stimulant that improves cognition, alertness and focus. As it has been stated from two recent scientific research studies. One that was published in September of 2014 titled, *"Dual role of nicotine in addiction and cognition: A review of neuroimaging studies in humans."* The other, published June of 2010 titled, *"Meta-analysis of the acute effects of nicotine and smoking on human performance."*

So let's summarize the liquid once again. Vaping liquid is comprised of Propylene Glycol (PG) and Vegetable Glycerin (VG). Both have been scientifically proven that the vapor not only cleans the air of bacteria, but also helps prevent respiratory infection. No problem with the clean air act here. Next ingredient is Nicotine. Something that is consumed by every human through certain types of vegetables and may reduce or prevent the effects of Parkinson's Disease. Nicotine is a performance-enhancing stimulant that improves cognition, alertness and focus. Again, doesn't sound like evil here. Lastly, artificial flavoring. It may not be the best thing to consume, but it doesn't kill anyone either.

Now that we know the vaporizer is an old technology that does not pose a health risk to anyone. And in fact, has been a health remedy for 134 years. It makes a person wonder why health organizations across the globe are trying to put bans on the device that helps people quit smoking.

Do they just lack the knowledge? Are they really concerned with the health effects? Or is there some politically motivated reason why they want the vaporizer placed under bans?

THE POLITICS OF VAPING

I understand the need for laws. However, it is deplorable that the people, and the political organizations that hold so much influence—just simply do not care to educate themselves before affecting millions of lives.

A recent prime example of this is California State Senator Mark Leno. He recently made the statement, *"No tobacco product should be exempt from California's smoke-free laws simply because it's sold in a modern or trendy disguise. Addiction is what's really being sold. Like traditional cigarettes, e-cigarettes deliver nicotine in a cloud of other toxic chemicals, and their use should be restricted equally under state law in order to protect public health."*

Mr. Leno has introduced a bill to treat e-cigarettes and vaporizers just like tobacco cigarettes. Let's take a closer look at Mr. Leno's statement. In his first three words he says, *"No tobacco product,"* this is simple ignorance. Vaporizers or e-cigarettes are not tobacco products. It is more a Nicotine product.

Here's the definition of Nicotine as per Medical News Today : *Nicotine is a nitrogen-containing chemical - an alkaloid, which is made by several types of plants, including the tobacco plant.*

Nicotine is also produced synthetically.

Nicotiana tabacum, the type of nicotine found in tobacco plants, comes from the nightshade family. Red peppers, eggplant, tomatoes and potatoes are examples of the nightshade family. So should we ban things like tomatoes and potatoes since they also contain nicotine? Let's continue to look at Mr. Leno's statement where he states, "*Addiction is what's really being sold.*" That maybe true and maybe it's the nicotine in pizza that has caused the record number of obesity cases. The nicotine in the tomato sauce has people addicted to pizza. So should we ban pizza?

The truth is the human race is an addictive being. Everyone is an addict, yes, EVERYONE. People are addicted to breathing oxygen, drinking water, and eating. There is nothing wrong with being addicted to a product that helps clean the bacteria out of the air and may prevent a disease like Parkinson's.

Then there is the obvious mistake that is made by smokers, non smokers, politicians, lawmakers, health organizations, and sadly enough even vapor shop owners. E-cigarettes and vaporizers are completely two different beasts. "What?!" I can hear you screaming. That's right. The two products are completely different and here's why. E-cigarettes have a nicotine cartridge. Inside that cartridge is nicotine soaked…wait for it…POLYFILL. What is polyfill? Polyfill is a stuffing made from polyester. A synthetic fiber made from polymers. A vaporizer however, uses natural and organic cotton. The research that has been done on e-cigarettes found some toxins, probably due to the polyfill. But the e-cigarette toxins were still 450 times less than that of a normal cigarette. The vaporizer has no toxins. Remember the vaporizer up until 2009 has had only one use for 134 years— to improve the health of humans worldwide. But all of the push to ban vaporizers and the like; might be something much more simpler.

There are three theories that make sense, well sort of. The first is the Big Tobacco theory.

Some people believe that the Big Tobacco companies are pushing to have the vaporizers banned because they are losing money and customers. Almost overnight the vaping industry grew to millions of ex-smokers. Some theorize that Big Tobacco may even finance some of the smoke free organizations, in hopes to coerce them, to include vaporizers in the smoke free bans. The whole stupidity of the organizations is that all of them use the same two words, "*Smoke Free.*" A person with common sense would realize that smoke is not created with a vaporizer. To this day there is not one organization in the world that uses the term, "*Vapor free.*" If they did then Vick's might have to pull their vaporizers off the shelf, but then, Proctor & Gamble might have a problem with that. All the organizations and politicians still have not realized vaping is not smoking.

The second theory has Big Bad Pharmaceutical companies trying to huff and puff vaporizers out of existence. Some people believe that Big Pharm has been lobbying and investing in smoke free organizations to put bans on smoking to help their smoking cessation products. The pharmaceutical companies have literally made billions off of nicotine patches, nicotine gum, and prescription medication to help smokers quit. Now imagine a better, healthier, version of the cigarette, that came to the rescue. That could successfully end their billion dollar business. Or would it?

Sometimes I wonder how these big time college graduates, some of them graduating from the finest business schools, had ever made it in business? Imagine if we could all get along. If Big Tobacco hopped on board the vape train. You could possibly see products like Camel Clouds, or Kool Klouds, featuring lime menthol vape juice. Or how about Marlboro invites you to…Vape Country.

And Big Pharmaceutical could start introducing ibuprofen that you could vape instead of swallow. Or how about a cough suppressant? Just a couple of drops and vape that cough away! These guys are failing to give it the ol' college try.

The third theory also makes a lot of sense. The theory is that local lawmakers are trying to show that e-cigarettes and vaporizers are similar to cigarettes by placing them under the smoke free bans. This way, it helps them to place heavy taxes on e-cigarettes, eLiquid, and the equipment as well. Because the more people that quit smoking by switching to vaporizers, the more tax money they lose from the purchase of tobacco products.

Too bad I'm not a lawyer. I would make the lawmakers, in cities that try to ban vaporizers, look like idiots. The future of vaporizers is looking bleak. Everyday more and more cities are trying to place vaporizers under their version of the smoke free bans. Now people are starting to see *"No Vaping"* signs placed in business windows.

All of this created due to ignorance and the failure of organizations not doing the research. A good example of this comes from the Respiratory Health Association of all people. This statement was an introduction of a report they had wrote concerning how kids are being exposed to electronic cigarettes.

"Electronic cigarettes (e-cigarettes) have grown dramatically in popularity over the last half-decade. As e-cigarette popularity has risen, so have rates of youth e-cigarette usage. A September, 2013 report by the U.S. Centers for Disease Control and Prevention reported that youth use of e-cigarettes doubled between 2011 and 2012. E-cigarettes are available in a large variety of sweet flavors, can be sold in youth-accessible locations, and can be widely advertised without running afoul of tobacco advertising restrictions. These factors have caused concern in the public health community that e-cigarettes may be a gateway for youth nicotine addiction and/or traditional tobacco use, and may act to "re-normalize" cigarette use as a social norm. While there is great concern over youth exposure to e-cigarettes, little is known about the long-term health effects of e-cigarette use. The U.S. Food and Drug Administration (FDA) is currently assessing the impact of e- cigarettes and plans to announce proposed regulations in late 2013. Until the FDA proposals are announced, e-cigarette regulation will only exist at the state and local level. The purpose of this paper is to provide local health officials and policy makers a concise summary of the public health concerns and potential policy solutions regarding e-cigarettes. The public health issues highlighted by the paper include: increased youth use and exposure to e-cigarettes; the unknown health effects of long-term e-cigarette use; the lack of universal product standards; and the devices' unknown efficacy as a cessation tool. Finally, the paper examines the current state of e-cigarette regulation and outlines several potential local policy options."

Little is known about the long term health effects? Obviously they did not do their research before writing this report, that was published in November of 2013. It doesn't make sense why a respiratory health organization would want to ban a product that prevents respiratory infection.

Furthermore, it's this type of thinking, that twenty-four states Attorney Generals wanted the FDA to ban flavors of eLiquid. The idea stems from the "let's save the children," argument. The type of kids that vapor prevented 132 of them from getting respiratory infection.

Then they'll try to drop the Diacetyl bomb. If your not familiar with the whole "Popcorn Lung" argument here it is in a nutshell. Diacetyl is a chemical that is used to flavor many food items like margarine, popcorn, coffee, just to name a few. The problem came up when people realized that eLiquids had been using the chemical in their flavorings as well. This would not have been a problem except, in 1990 a few workers who had worked in a microwave popcorn production plant, came down with bronchiolitis, a serious respiratory illness. Scientist believed that Diacetyl was the main culprit for the workers ailment. Soon the ailment was coined the term *Popcorn Lung*. However they could never prove that the Diacetyl was the actual cause, since the powder the workers had inhaled for so many years, also had a hundred other questionable chemicals. But the lawmakers still bring this point up, even though, most if not all eLiquid artificial flavor manufacturers have stop using Diacetyl all together. The lawmakers also ignore the fact that a report from, Critical Reviews in Toxicology, that stated, *"Smoking has not been shown to be a risk factor for bronchiolitis (popcorn lung)."* This is important because it had been proven that, when eLiquid artificial flavoring did contain Diacetyl, cigarette smokers had been exposed to the chemical 750 times higher than a person vaping.

The stupidity isn't just remaining in the United States.

It's spreading like a pandemic. In May of 2016 England will start enforcing such idiot regulations as limiting the size of eLiquid bottles to ten milliliters, limiting atomizer tanks to two milliliters, and eliminating twenty-four milligram nicotine eLiquids. But here's the topper. They want to require that vaporizers have to deliver a constant dose of nicotine. How is that even possible?

Society has successfully caused the majority to quit smoking, but that doesn't mean they don't miss it. What makes the vaporizer nice is being able to get your nicotine fix without people around you whining about it. You can vape anywhere without fear of health risks. With the vaporizer—the days of smoking in a restaurant, bar, hospital, movie theater, or airplane should be back.

The only way to keep cigarettes and vaporizers separate, as they should be, will be to vote the lawmakers out of office. Then ensuring any lawmaker, that does not have the vapor users best interest, will not be elected again. This industry needs one and only one organization that can rally the votes of every vapor user in America.

Then there is an even darker cloud on the horizon. There are organizations that are only concerned with the vapor shop owners. They are wasting their time and energy with trying to fight legislation concerning regulations that impose child safety caps on eLiquid. They are worried that there will be extra costs equalling less profit for them. Child safety caps should be on every bottle of eLiquid. That's just common sense. These organizations need to concentrate on preventing bans on vaporizers under the clean air or smoke free laws.

Also now there are some eLiquid manufacturers who are trying to replace Propylene Glycol with an ingredient called Propanediol. These brainiacs want to take the one ingredient that has been scientifically proven to kill airborne bacteria, prevent respiratory infections, and replace it with an ingredient that does nothing beneficial health wise. Humans never want to, "just leave shit alone."

This is why I fear that the dimwitted lawmakers and organizations like American Nonsmokers Rights Foundation will prevail.

THE LAWS OF VAPING

Let's take a look thus far all the laws in each state as it pertains to electronic cigarettes and vaporizers. These are the laws as of October 2015 and what each state defines as a electronic cigarette. Or what some states has dubbed Alternative Nicotine Product. It also shows cities within each state that has included vaporizers in their smoke free ban.

Alabama

Definition: *ALTERNATIVE NICOTINE PRODUCT. The term alternative nicotine product includes electronic cigarettes. An electronic cigarette is an electronic product or device that produces a vapor that delivers nicotine or other substances to the person inhaling from the device to simulate smoking, and is likely to be offered to, or purchased by, consumers as an electronic cigarette, electronic cigar, electronic cigarillo, or electronic pipe.*

State Laws: *Unlawful for minors to purchase, use, possess, or transport tobacco, tobacco product, or alternative nicotine product.*

State Smoke Free Laws: None

Cities that include vaporizers in their Smoke Free Laws: Anniston, Bessemer, Clay, Creola, Foley,

Fultondale, Gadsden, Midfiedld, Monroeville, Opelika, Troy, and Vestavia Hills.

Alaska
Definition: None
State Laws: *Unlawful to sell or give "product containing nicotine" to person under age 19.*
State Smoke Free Laws: None
Cities that include vaporizers in their Smoke Free Laws: Dillingham, Juneau, and Palmer.

Arizona
Definition: *Vapor Product means a "noncombustible tobacco-derived product containing nicotine that employs a mechanical heating element, battery or circuit, regardless of shape or size that can be used to heat a liquid nicotine solution contained in cartridges."*
State Laws: 1. *Unlawful to sell vapor product to minor; unlawful for minor to purchase or possess vapor product.*

2. *Sale/distribution of e-cigarettes to persons under age 18 is prohibited.*
State Smoke Free Laws: *Use of e-cigarettes near schools or on school buses.*
Cities that include vaporizers in their Smoke Free Laws: Coconino County and Tempe.

Arkansas
Definition: 1. *E-cigarette means "an electronic oral device that provides a vapor of nicotine or another substance that, when used or inhaled, simulates smoking, including without limitation a device that (A) is composed of a heating element, battery, electronic circuit, or a combination of heating element, battery, or electronic circuit; (B) works in combination with a liquid nicotine delivery device composed either, in whole or in part, of pure nicotine and manufactured for use with e-cigarettes; and (C) is manufactured, distributed, marketed or sold as an e-cigarette, e- cigar, e-pipe, or under any other product*

name or descriptor..."

2. *Electronic Cigarette means "an electronic product or device that produces a vapor that delivers nicotine or another substance to the person inhaling from the device to simulate smoking, and that is likely to be offered to or purchased by consumers as an electronic cigarette, electronic cigar, electronic cigarillo, or electronic pipe."*

3. *Alternative Nicotine Product includes Electronic Cigarettes.*

State Laws: 1. *Sale/distribution of e-cigarettes to persons under age 18.*

2. *Distribution of e-cigarettes or coupons for e-cigarettes to minors or near playgrounds schools or other areas frequented by minors.*

3. *Possession/purchase of e-cigarettes by persons under age 18 prohibited.*

4. *No self-service displays of e- cigarettes in locations accessible to minors.*

State Smoke Free Laws: 1. *Use of e-cigarettes near schools or on school buses prohibited.*

2. *Use of e-cigarettes in registered day- care facilities prohibited.*

Cities that include vaporizers in their Smoke Free Laws: None

California

Definition: *Electronic Cigarette means "a device that can provide an inhalable does of nicotine by delivering a vaporized solution."*

State Laws: *Sale of electronic cigarettes to persons under age 18 prohibited.*

State Smoke Free Laws: *No school shall permit smoking or use of tobacco or any product containing tobacco or nicotine products by students.*

Cities that include vaporizers in their Smoke Free Laws: Arcata, Artesia, Berkeley, Beverly Hills, Calabasas, Camarillo, Campbell, Capitola, Carlsbad,

Chico, Contra Costa County, Corte Madera, Daly City, Davis, Del Mar, Dixon Dublin, El Cajon, El Cerrito, Eureka, Fairfax, Folsom, Foster City, Fremont, Garden Grove, Goleta, Hayward, Laguna Hills, Lemon Grove, Lompoc, Long Beach, Los Angeles, Mammoth Lakes, Manhattan Beach, Marin County, Mill Valley, Morgan Hill, Mountain View, Oroville, Paradise, Petaluma, Pico Rivera, Pittsburg, Pleasant Hill, Pleasanton, Rancho Cordova, Richmond, San Anselmo, San Bernardino County, San Diego, San Diego County, San Francisco, San Luis Obispo, San Mateo County, Santa Barbara County, Santa Clara, Santa Clara County, Santa Cruz, Santa Maria, Santa Monica, Santa Rosa, Scotts Valley, Seal Beach, Sebastopol, Shasta County, Solana Beach, Solano County, Solvang, Sonoma County, Temecula, Tiburon, Union City, Ventura, Walnut Creek, and Watsonville.

Colorado

Definition: *Cigarette, Tobacco Product or Nicotine Product means "(i) a product that contains nicotine or tobacco or is derived from tobacco and is intended to be ingested or inhaled by or applied to the skin of an individual; or (ii) any device that can be used to deliver tobacco or nicotine to the person inhaling from the device, including an electronic cigarette, cigar, cigarillo or pipe."*

State Laws: 1. *Furnishing cigarettes, tobacco products, or nicotine products to minors.*

2. *Possession or purchase of e- cigarettes by persons under age 18 prohibited.*

State Smoke Free Laws: 1. *Use of e-cigarettes prohibited on school grounds.*

2. *Use of nicotine products in and around licensed child care*

facilities prohibited.

Cities that include vaporizers in their Smoke Free Laws: Arvada, Boulder, Breckenridge, Brighton, Edgewater, Evans, Fort Collins, Frisco, Golden, Greeley, Lafayette, Lakewood, and Louisville.

Connecticut

Definition: 1. *Electronic Nicotine Delivery System means "an electronic device that may be used to simulate smoking in the delivery of nicotine or other substance to a person inhaling from the device, and includes, but is not limited to, an electronic cigarette, electronic cigar, electronic cigarillo, electronic pipe or electronic hookah and any related device and any cartridge or other component of such device."*

2. Vapor Product means "any product that employs a heating element, power source, electronic circuit or other electronic, chemical or mechanical means, regardless of shape or size, to produce a vapor that may or may not include nicotine, that is inhaled by the user of such product."

State Laws: 1. *Sale/delivery of electronic nicotine delivery system or vapor product to persons under age 18 prohibited.*

2. Purchase/possession of electronic nicotine delivery system or vapor product by persons under age 18 prohibited.

State Smoke Free Laws: None

Cities that include vaporizers in their Smoke Free Laws: None

Delaware

Definition: *Tobacco Substitute means "any device employing a mechanical heating element, battery, or circuit, regardless of shape or size, that can be used to deliver nicotine into the body through inhalation ..., or any noncombustible product containing nicotine intended for use in such a device ..."*

State Laws: 1. *Sale/distribution of tobacco substitutes to persons under age 18 prohibited.*

2. *Purchase of tobacco substitutes by persons under age 18 prohibited.*

3. *Self-service displays of tobacco substitutes prohibited in places accessible to persons under age 18.*

State Smoke Free Laws: None

Cities that include vaporizers in their Smoke Free Laws: None

District of Columbia

Definition: *E-cigarette means "an electronic vaporizer that produces an aerosol that simulates tobacco smoking."*

State Laws: None

State Smoke Free Laws: None

Cities that include vaporizers in their Smoke Free Laws: None

Florida

Definition: 1. *Nicotine Dispensing Device means "any product that employs an electronic, chemical, or mechanical means to produce vapor from a nicotine product, including, but not limited to, an electronic cigarette, electronic cigar, electronic cigarillo, electronic pipe, or other similar device or product, any replacement cartridge for such device, and any other container of nicotine in a solution or other form intended to be used with or within an electronic cigarette, electronic cigar, electronic cigarillo, electronic pipe, or other similar device or product."*

2. *Nicotine Product means "any product that contains nicotine, including liquid nicotine, that is intended for human consumption, whether inhaled, chewed, absorbed, dissolved, or ingested by any means, but does not include a: (1) Tobacco product, as defined in § 569.002..."*

State Laws: 1. *Sale/distribution of nicotine dispensing devices or nicotine products to persons under age 18 years prohibited.*

2. *Possession of nicotine dispensing devices or nicotine products by*

persons under age 18 prohibited.

3. *Self-service displays of nicotine products or nicotine dispensing devices prohibited in places accessible to persons under 18 years except when under direct control or line of sight of retailer, or sales made through vending machine with lockout device controlled by retailer.* **State Smoke Free Laws:** None

Cities that include vaporizers in their Smoke Free Laws: Alachua County, Archer, Belleview, Boca Raton, Clay County, Delray Beach, Gainesville, Hawthorne, High Springs, Lighthouse Point, Marion County, Miami/Dade County, NewBerry, Orange Park, Port Saint Lucie, Port Saint Joe, Vero Beach, and Waldo.

Georgia

Definition: 1. *Alternative Nicotine Product means "any noncombustible product containing nicotine that is intended for human consumption, whether chewed, absorbed, dissolved, or ingested by any other means."*

2. *Vapor Product means "any noncombustible product containing nicotine that employs a heating element, power source, electronic circuit, or other electronic, chemical, or mechanical means, regardless of shape or size, that can be used to produce vapor from nicotine in a solution or other form. The term "vapor product" shall include any electronic cigarette, electronic cigar, electronic cigarillo, electronic pipe, or similar product or device and any vapor cartridge or other container of nicotine in a solution or other form that is intended to be used with or in an electronic cigarette, electronic cigar, electronic cigarillo, electronic pipe, or similar product or device."*

State Laws: 1. Sale of alternative nicotine products or vapor products to persons under age 18 prohibited.

2. *Distribution of alternative nicotine products to general public or to persons under the age 18 prohibited.*

3. *Purchase/possession of alternative nicotine products or vapor*

products by persons under age 18 prohibited.

State Smoke Free Laws: None

Cities that include vaporizers in their Smoke Free Laws: Chatham County, DeKalb County, Pooler, and Savannah.

Hawaii

Definition: 1. *The following definition applies to youth access law: Electronic Smoking Device means "any electronic product that can be used to simulate smoking in the delivery of nicotine or other substances to the person inhaling from the device, including but not limited to an electronic cigarette, electronic cigar, electronic cigarillo, or electronic pipe, and any cartridge or other component of the device or related product."*

2. The following definitions apply to smoking restrictions: Electronic Smoking Device means "any electronic product that can be used to aerosolize and deliver nicotine or other substances to the person inhaling from the device, including but not limited to an electronic cigarette, electronic cigar, electronic cigarillo, electronic pipe, hookah pipe, or hookah pen, and any cartridge or other component of the device or related product, whether or not sold separately."

3. Tobacco Product means "any product made or derived from tobacco, that contains nicotine or other substances, and is intended for human consumption or is likely to be consumed, whether smoked, heated, chewed, absorbed, dissolved, inhaled, or ingested by any other means, including, but not limited to, a cigarette, cigar, pipe tobacco, chewing tobacco, snuff, snus, or an electronic smoking device..."

State Laws: 1. *Sale/distribution of electronic smoking devices to persons under age 18 prohibited.*

2. Purchase of electronic smoking device by person under age 18 prohibited.

State Smoke Free Laws: *Use of electronic smoking devices prohibited in enclosed or partially enclosed places that are: owned,* leased or operated by the state or counties, open to the public, places of employment, sports arenas/stadiums, and within *"presumptive reasonable distance"* of entrances and exits to such places.

Cities that include vaporizers in their Smoke Free Laws: Hawaii County

Idaho

Definition: *Electronic Cigarette means "any device that can provide an inhaled dose of nicotine by delivering a vaporized solution. 'Electronic cigarette' includes the components of an electronic cigarette including, but not limited to, liquid nicotine"*

State Laws: *1. Sale/distribution of electronic cigarettes to minors prohibited.*

2. Possession/purchase/distribution/u se of electronic cigarettes by minors prohibited.

3. Vending machine sales and self- service displays of electronic cigarettes restricted to adult-only tobacco stores.

4. If shipping e-cigarettes, seller required to obtain proof of age.

5. Shipment of e-cigarettes must include statement re: prohibition on shipping to individuals under age 18.

State Smoke Free Laws: None

Cities that include vaporizers in their Smoke Free Laws: Ketchum

Illinois

Definition: 1. *Electronic Cigarette or E- Cigarette means "a battery- operated device that contains a combination of nicotine, flavor, or chemicals or any combination thereof that are turned into vapor which is inhaled by the user."*

2. *Alternative Nicotine Product means "a product or device not consisting of or containing tobacco that provides for the ingestion into the body of nicotine, whether by chewing, smoking, absorbing, dissolving, inhaling, snorting, sniffing or by any other means."*

State Laws: 1. *Electronic cigarette liquids may be sold only in* *child-resistant packaging pursuant to rules adopted by the Department of Public Health, excluding e-cigarette products sold in "sealed, pre- filled, or disposable replacement cartridges."*

2. Distribution of alternative nicotine products to or by persons under age 18 prohibited.

3. Self-service display of alternative nicotine products restricted to adult-only tobacco stores.

State Smoke Free Laws: *Use of products containing nicotine prohibited on public higher education campuses.*

Cities that include vaporizers in their Smoke Free Laws: Arlington Heights, Chicago, Deerfield, DeKalb, Elk Grove Village, Evanston, Naperville, Oak Park, Ogle County, Schaumburg, Skokie, and Wilmette.

Indiana

Definition: 1. *Electronic Cigarette means "a device that is capable of providing an inhalable dose of nicotine by delivering a vaporized solution. The term includes the components and cartridges.*

2. Electronic Delivery Device means "any product that: (1) contains or delivers nicotine, lobelia, or any other substance intended for human consumption; and (2) can be used by a person to simulate smoking in the delivery of nicotine, lobelia, or any other substance through inhalation of vapor from the product...[and] includes any component part...whether or not the component part is marketed or sold separately."

State Laws: 1. *Nicotine liquid must be sold in child-resistant packaging, excluding pre- filled, sealed and not intended to be opened by consumer.*

2. Sale/distribution of electronic cigarettes to persons under age 18 prohibited.

3. Possession/purchase of electronic cigarettes by persons under age 18 prohibited.

4. *Self-service displays of electronic cigarettes restricted to adult-only tobacco stores.*

5. *Retailers of electronic cigarettes must be registered.*

State Smoke Free Laws: None

Cities that include vaporizers in their Smoke Free Laws: Greenwood and Indianapolis/Marion

Iowa

Definitions: 1. *Vapor product means "any noncombustible product, which may or may not contain nicotine, that employs a heating element, power source, electronic circuit, or other electronic, chemical, or mechanical means, regardless of shape or size, that can be used to produce vapor from a solution or other substance. 'Vapor product' includes an electronic cigarette, electronic cigar, electronic cigarillo, electronic pipe, or similar product or device, and any cartridge or other container of a solution or other substance, which may or may not contain nicotine, that is intended to be used with or in an electronic cigarette, electronic cigar, electronic cigarillo, electronic pipe, or similar product or device."*

2. *Alternative nicotine product means "a product, not consisting of or containing tobacco, that provides for the ingestion into the body of nicotine, whether by chewing, absorbing, dissolving, inhaling, snorting, or sniffing, or by any other means. 'Alternative nicotine product' does not include cigarettes, tobacco products, or vapor products.*

State Laws: 1. *Sale/distribution of vapor products or alternative nicotine products to anyone under age 18 prohibited.*

2. *Possession/purchase of alternative nicotine products or vapor products by persons under age 18 prohibited.*

3. *Retailers must obtain a permit before selling vapor products.*

4. *No distribution of free vapor products or alternative nicotine products to persons under age 18 or within 500 feet of places primarily used by minors.*

5. *Self-service displays prohibited.*
6. *Vending machine sales restricted to adult-only locations.*
State Smoke Free Laws: None
Cities that include vaporizers in their Smoke Free Laws: Iowa City

Kansas
Definition: *Electronic Cigarette means "a battery-powered device, whether or not such device is shaped like a cigarette, that can provide inhaled doses of nicotine by delivering a vaporized solution by means of cartridges or other chemical delivery systems."*

State Laws: 1. *Sale/distribution of electronic cigarettes to persons under age 18 prohibited.*

2. *Purchase/possession of electronic cigarettes by person under age 18 prohibited.*

3. *Self-service displays of electronic cigarettes restricted to tobacco specialty stores and vending machine inaccessible to minors or which has a lock-out device.*

4. *Retailers of electronic cigarettes must obtain a license.*

State Smoke Free Laws: None

Cities that include vaporizers in their Smoke Free laws: Kansas City, Wyandotte, Olathe, Overland Park, Park City, and Topeka.

Kentucky
Definition: 1. *Vapor Product means "any noncombustible product that employs a heating element, battery, power source, electronic circuit, or other electronic, chemical, or mechanical means, regardless of shape or size and including the component parts and accessories thereto, that can be used to deliver vaporized nicotine or other substances to users inhaling from the device. 'Vapor product' includes but is not limited to any electronic cigarette, electronic cigar, electronic cigarillo, electronic pipe, or similar product or device and every variation thereof, regardless of whether marketed as such, and*

any vapor cartridge or other container of a liquid solution or other material that is intended to be used with or in an electronic cigarette, electronic cigar, electronic cigarillo, electronic pipe, or other similar product or device."

2. *Alternative Nicotine Product means "a noncombustible product containing nicotine that is intended for human consumption, whether chewed, absorbed, dissolved, or ingested by other means."*

State Laws: 1. *Sale of vapor products or alternative nicotine product to persons under age 18 prohibited.*

2. *Purchase of vapor products or alternative nicotine products by persons under age 18 prohibited*

3. *Possession/use of vapor products or alternative nicotine products by person under age 18 prohibited.*

4. *Distribution of free vapor products or alternative nicotine products to persons under age 18 years prohibited.*

5. *Vending machine sales of vapor products and alternative nicotine products to persons under 18 prohibited.*

State Smoke Free Laws: None

Cities that include vaporizers in their Smoke Free Laws: Bardstown, Berea, Danville, Glasgow, Lexington, Fayette, Manchester, Morehead, Richmond, Versailles, and Woodford County.

Louisiana

Definition: 1. *Vapor Product means "any non-combustible product containing nicotine or other substances that employs a heating element, power source, electronic circuit, or other electronic, chemical or mechanical means, regardless of shape or size, that can be used to produce vapor from nicotine in a solution or other form. 'Vapor product' includes any electronic cigarette, electronic cigar, electronic cigarillo, electronic pipe, or similar product or device and any vapor cartridge or other container of nicotine in a solution or other form that is intended to be used with or in an electronic cigarette, electronic* *cigar, electronic cigarillo, electronic pipe, or similar product or device."*

2. Alternative Nicotine Product means "any non- combustible product containing nicotine that is intended for human consumption, whether chewed, absorbed, dissolved, or ingested by any other means...[but] does not include any ... vapor product."

State Laws: 1.*Sale/distribution of vapor products or alternative nicotine products to persons under age 18 prohibited.*

2. Purchase or possession of vapor product or alternative nicotine product by persons under age 18 prohibited unless accompanied by parent or in a private residence.

3. Self-service displays of vapor products and alternative nicotine products restricted to tobacco businesses and vending machines located in age-restricted settings.

4. Permits required for retailers of vapor products and alternative nicotine products.

State Smoke Free Laws: None

Cities that include vaporizers in their Smoke Free Laws: Abbeville, Cheneyville, Hammond, Monroe, New Orleans, Ouachita Parish, Sulphur, and West Monroe.

Maine
Definition: None
State Laws: None
State Smoke Free Laws: None
Cities that include vaporizers in their Smoke Free Laws: None

Maryland
Definition: None
State Laws: *Sale of "an electronic device that can be used to deliver nicotine to the individual inhaling from the device, including an electronic cigarette, cigar, cigarillo, or pipe" to minors prohibited*

(excluding FDA approved medical devices).
State Smoke Free Laws: None
Cities that include vaporizers in their Smoke Free Laws: Baltimore and Montgomery County.
Massachusetts
Definition: None
State Laws: None
State Smoke Free Laws: None
Cities that include vaporizers in their Smoke Free Laws: Acton, Adams, Amherst, Andover, Arlington, Athol, Auburn, Barre, Billerica, Boltoon, Boston, Bourne, Bridgeater, Buckland, Burlington, Cambridge, Cohasset, Concord, Dartmouth, Dedham, Deerfield, Dighton, Dover, Dracut, Eastham, Easthampton, Fairhaven, Fitchburg, Foxborough, Franklin, Gardner, Gill, Grafton, Grany, Great Barrington, Greenfield, Hamilton, Hatfield, Haverhill, Holyoke, Hubbardston, Hudson, Hull, Lee, Leicester, Lenox, Leominster, Leverett, Lynn, Lynnfield, Marblehead, Marlborough, Marshfield, Mashpee, Medway, Methuen, Milford, Montague, Needham, New Bedford, Newburyport, Newton, North Andover, North Attleborough, North Reading, Northampton, Orange, Orleans, Oxford, Pittsfield, Plainville, Provincetown, Salem, Saugus, Sharon, Shelburne, Sherborn, Somerset, South Hadley, Stockbridge, Sunderland, Sutton, Swampscott, Taunton, Tewksbury, Townsend, Wakefield, Watertown, Wayland, Webster, Wendell, West Springfield, Westminster, Westport, Westwood, Weymouth, Whately, Williamstown, Winchendon, and Winchester.
Michigan
Definition: None
State Laws: None

State Smoke Free Laws: None
Cities that include vaporizers in their Smoke Free Laws: Washtenaw County.
Minnesota
Definition: *Electronic delivery device means "any product containing or delivering nicotine, lobelia, or any other substance intended for human consumption that can be used by a person to simulate smoking in the delivery of nicotine or any other substance through inhalation of vapor from the product. Electronic delivery device includes any component part of a product, whether or not marketed or sold separately..."*

State Laws: 1. *Tax of 95% of wholesale price imposed on tobacco products, including e- cigarettes.*

2. Liquids intended for human consumption and use in an electronic delivery device (whether contain nicotine or not) must be sold in child resistant packaging.

3. Sale/distribution of electronic delivery devices prohibited to persons under age 18.

4. Purchase/possession of electronic delivery device by person under age 18 prohibited.

5. Sale of electronic delivery devices from a moveable place of business (kiosk) prohibited.

6. Self-service displays of electronic delivery devices restricted to adult- only tobacco businesses and vending machines in locations inaccessible to persons under age 18.

State Smoke Free Laws: 1. *Use of electronic delivery devices prohibited in day care and health facilities, and certain publicly- owned buildings.*

2. Use of electronic delivery devices prohibited in public schools and any facility or vehicle owned, rented or leased by the school district.

Cities that include vaporizers in their Smoke

Free Laws: Austin, Beltrami County, Big Stone County, Bloomington, Duluth, Eagle Lake, Eden Prairie, Edina, Ely, Hennepin county, Hermantown, Houston County, Isanti, Jordan, Lakeville, Mankato, Marshall County, Minneapolis, Moorhead, North Mankato, Olmsted County, Orono, Savage, Sleepy Eye, St. Anthony, St. Louis County, and Waseca.

Mississippi
Definition: 1. *Alternative Nicotine Product means "(1) An electronic cigarette; or (2) Any other product that consists of or contains nicotine that can be ingested into the body by chewing, smoking, absorbing, dissolving, inhaling or by any other means.*

2. Electronic Cigarette means "an electronic product or device that produces a vapor that delivers nicotine or other substances to the person inhaling from the device to stimulate smoking, and is likely to be offered to, or purchased by, consumers as an electronic cigarette, electronic cigar, electronic cigarillo or electronic pipe."

State Laws: 1. *Sale of alternative nicotine products or any cartridge or component to persons under 18 prohibited.*

2. Internet sales of alternative nicotine products require age verification.

State Smoke Free Laws: None

Cities that include vaporizers in their Smoke Free Laws: Anguilla, Arcola, Baldwyn, Bassfield, Beulah, Brandon, Bruce, Byram, Calhoun City, Centreville, Coahoma County, Courtland, Crawford, Duck Hill, Duncan, Durant, Ethel, Farmington, Fayette, Flowood, Forest, Friars Point, Georgetown, Holly Springs, Indianola, Isola, Itta Bena, Iuka, Louisville, Magee, Mantachie, Mendenhall, Monticello, Moorhead, Nettleton, New Augusta, petal, Pickens, Pittsboro,

Plantersville, Prentiss, Rolling Fork, Saltillo, Sidon, Sledge, Southaven, State Line, Sumner, Tupelo, Tutwiler, Walnut, Walnut Grove, Weir, Wesson, and Woodville.

Missouri

Definition: 1. *Alternative Nicotine Product means "any non-combustible product containing nicotine that is intended for human consumption, whether chewed, absorbed, dissolved, or ingested by any other means. 'Alternative nicotine product' does not include any vapor product..."*

2. *Vapor Product means "any non-combustible product containing nicotine that employs a heating element, power source, electronic circuit ... [including] the container of nicotine in a solution or other form... "Vapor products does not include any alternative nicotine product or tobacco product."*

State Laws: 1. *Sale of alternative nicotine products or vapor products to persons under age 18 prohibited.*

2. *Mail and internet sales of alternative nicotine or vapor products to persons under 18 prohibited.*

3. *Vending machines that sell these products "shall be located within the unobstructed line of sight and under the direct supervision of an adult responsible for preventing persons less than 18 year of age from purchasing ..." Vending machines also shall be equipped with a lock-out device, and the default is in the locked position.*

4. *Purchase of alternative nicotine products or vapor products by persons less than age 18 prohibited.*

5. *Retailers must obtain retail sales tax license.*

State Smoke Free Laws: None

Cities that include vaporizers in their Smoke Free Laws: Branson, Clinton, Columbia, Creve,Coeur, Gainesville, St. Joseph, and Washington.

Montana

Definition: 1. *Alternative nicotine product means "any* *manufactured noncombustible product containing nicotine derived from tobacco that is intended for human consumption, whether chewed, absorbed, dissolved, or ingested by any other means. 'Alternative nicotine product' does not include any vapor product..."*

2. Vapor Product means a non-combustible product that may contain nicotine and that uses a heating element, power source, electronic circuit, or other electronic, chemical, or mechanical means, regardless of shape or size, to produce vapor from a solution or other substance. The term includes an electronic cigarette, electronic cigar, electronic cigarillo, electronic pipe, or similar product or device and a vapor cartridge or other container that may contain nicotine in a solution or other form that is intended to be used with or in an electronic cigarette, electronic cigar, electronic cigarillo, electronic pipe, or similar product or device...."

State Laws: 1. *Retailers must obtain license.*

2. *Sale/distribution of alternative nicotine products or vapor products to persons under age 18 prohibited.*

3. *Vending machine sales restricted to bars where machine is under direct line-of-sight supervision.*

4. *Possession/use of alternative nicotine products or vapor products by persons under age 18 prohibited.*

State Smoke Free Laws: None

Cities that include vaporizers in their Smoke Free Laws: Lewis and Clark County

Nebraska

Definition: 1. *Alternative Nicotine Products means "any noncombustible product containing nicotine that is intended for human consumption, whether chewed, absorbed, dissolved, or ingested by any other means. 'Alternative nicotine product' does not include any vapor product . . ."*

2. *Vapor Product means "any noncombustible product containing nicotine that employs a heating element, power source, electronic*

circuit, or other electronic, chemical, or mechanical means ... that can be used to produce vapor from nicotine in a solution or other form. Vapor Product includes any electronic cigarette, [cigar, cigarillo, pipe] or similar product or device."

State Laws: 1. *Sale/distribution of vapor products or alternative nicotine products to persons under age 18 prohibited.*

2. Use of vapor products or alternative nicotine products by persons under age 18 prohibited.

3. Vending machine sales of vapor products and alternative nicotine products are restricted to locations inaccessible to minors or an establishment that has a liquor license and which sells alcohol in the same room as the vending machine.

4. Self-service displays restricted to tobacco specialty stores and cigar bars.

State Smoke Free Laws: None

Cities that include vaporizers in their Smoke Free Laws: None

Nevada
Definition: None
State Laws: None
State Smoke Free Laws: None
Cities that include vaporizers in their Smoke Free Laws: None

New Hampshire
Definition: 1. *E-cigarette means "any electronic smoking device composed of a mouthpiece, a heating element, a battery, and electronic circuits that provides a vapor of pure nicotine mixed with propylene glycol to the user as the user simulates smoking. This term shall include such devices whether they are manufactured as e-cigarettes, e-cigars, or e- pipes, or under any other product name."*

2. Liquid Nicotine means "any liquid product composed either in whole or in part of pure nicotine and propylene glycol and

manufactured for use with e-cigarettes."

State Laws: 1. *Sale/distribution of e-cigarettes and liquid nicotine to minors prohibited.*

2. *Distribution of free e-cigarettes or liquid nicotine prohibited except in locations inaccessible to minors.*

3. *Purchase/possession of e-cigarettes or liquid nicotine by minors prohibited.*

State Smoke Free Laws: *Use of e-cigarette and liquid nicotine on public educational facility grounds prohibited.*

Cities that include vaporizers in their Smoke Free Laws: None

New Jersey

Definition: *Electronic Smoking Device means "an electronic device that can be used to deliver nicotine or other substances to the person inhaling from the device, including, but not limited to, an electronic cigarette, cigar, cigarillo, or pipe."*

State Laws: *Sale/distribution of electronic smoking device to person under age 19 prohibited.*

State Smoke Free Laws: *Use of electronic smoking device prohibited in indoor public places, workplaces and schools (with some exceptions).*

Cities that include vaporizers in their Smoke Free Laws: Newark

New Mexico

Definition: 1. *E-cigarette means "(1)... any electronic oral device, whether composed of a heating element and battery or an electronic circuit, that provides a vapor of nicotine or any other substances the use or inhalation of which simulates smoking; and (2) includes any such device, or any part thereof, whether manufactured, distributed, marketed or sold as an e- cigarette, e-cigar, e-pipe or any other product, name or descriptor...*

2. *Nicotine liquid container means "a bottle or other container of any substance containing nicotine where the substance is sold, marketed or intended for use in an e-cigarette."*

State Laws: 1. *Liquid nicotine must be sold in child-resistant container, excluding cartridges that are pre-filled and sealed by the manufacturer and not intended to be opened by the consumer.*

2. *E-cigarettes and nicotine liquid containers must be sold in original factory-sealed package.*

3. *Sale/distribution of e-cigarettes or a nicotine liquid container to persons under age 18 prohibited.*

4. *Procurement of e-cigarette or nicotine liquid container by persons under age 18 prohibited.*

5. *Internet sale of e-cigarettes or nicotine liquid containers to persons under age 18 in New Mexico is prohibited.*

6. *E-cigarettes and nicotine liquid containers may only be sold by a retailer face-to-face.*

7. *Self-service displays of e-cigarettes and nicotine liquid containers prohibited.*

8. *Vending machine sales are permitted only in adult-only locations.*

9. *Distribution of free e-cigarettes or nicotine liquid containers to persons under age 18 prohibited except in the practice of cultural or ceremonial activities in accordance with federal religious freedom act.*

State Smoke Free Laws: None

Cities that include vaporizers in their Smoke Free Laws: Carlsbad and Santa Fe.

New York
Definition: 1. *Electronic cigarette (or e- cigarette) means "an electronic device that delivers vapor which is inhaled by an individual user, and shall include any refill, cartridge and any other component of such a device."*

2. *Liquid nicotine (or electronic liquid or e- liquid) means "a liquid composed of nicotine and other chemicals, and which is sold as a product that may be used in an electronic cigarette."*

State Laws: 1. *Liquid nicotine must be sold in a child resistant bottle.*

2. *Sale/distribution of e-cigarettes or liquid nicotine to persons under age 18 prohibited.*

3. *Self service displays of e- cigarettes or liquid nicotine prohibited except in tobacco businesses.*

4. *Vending machine sales of e- cigarettes permitted in limited locations and must be visible to and under the direct control of person in charge.*

State Smoke Free Laws: None

Cities that include vaporizers in their Smoke Free Laws: Cattaraugus County, Lynbrook, New York City, Suffolk County, Tompkins County, and Westchester County.

North Carolina

Definition: 1. *Tobacco product includes "a tobacco-derived product, vapor product, or components of a vapor product."*

2. *Vapor product means "any noncombustible product that employs a mechanical heating element, battery, or electronic circuit regardless of shape or size and that can be used to heat a liquid nicotine solution contained in a vapor cartridge. The term includes an electronic cigarette."*

3. *Consumable product means "any nicotine liquid solution or other material containing nicotine that is depleted as a vapor product is used.*

State Laws: 1. *Vapor products taxed at rate of $0.05/fluid ml. of consumable product.*

2. *Sale/distribution of vapor products to persons under age 18 is prohibited.*

3. *Vending machine sales of vapor products restricted to locations inaccessible to minors where vending machine is under continuous control of owner and can be operated only upon activation by the owner.*

4. *Internet distribution of vapor products permitted with use of age verification through an independent, third-party service.*

5. *Purchase of vapor products by persons under age 18 prohibited.*

State Smoke Free Laws: *Vapor products prohibited on State correctional facilities premises, except for religious purposes.*

Cities that include vaporizers in their Smoke Free Laws: None

North Dakota

Definition: 1. *E-cigarette means "any electronic oral device, such as one composed of a heating element and battery or electronic circuit, or both, which provides a vapor of nicotine or any other substances, and the use or inhalation of which simulates smoking. The term shall include any such device, whether manufactured, distributed, marketed, or sold as an e- cigarette, e-cigar, and e- pipe or under any other product, name, or descriptor."*

2. *Electronic Smoking Device means "any electronic product that delivers nicotine or other substances to the individual inhaling from the device, including, an electronic cigarette, e- cigar, e-pipe, vape pen, or e-hookah. Electronic smoking device includes any component, part, or accessory of such a product, whether or not sold separately....."*

3. *Alternative Nicotine Product means "any noncombustible product containing nicotine that is intended for human consumption, whether chewed, absorbed, dissolved, or ingested by any other means. The term does not include any ... electronic smoking device...."*

State Laws: 1. *Nicotine liquid containers must be sold in child-resistant packaging, excepting pre- filled sealed containers not intended to be opened by consumers.*

2. *Sale/distribution of electronic smoking devices and alternative*

nicotine products to persons under age 18 prohibited.

3. Self-service displays restricted to tobacco specialty stores and vending machines inaccessible to minors or which are controlled by the seller.

4. Purchase/possession/use of electronic smoking device by person under age 18 prohibited.

5. Sales of electronic smoking devices by means other than face-to-face transactions restricted to retailers or persons whose age has been verified when product is shipped via method requiring signature of person verified to be at least age 18.

State Smoke Free Laws: *Use of e-cigarettes prohibited in public places and places of employment and within 20 feet of entrances, exits, windows, air intakes and ventilation systems thereof.*

Cities that include vaporizers in their Smoke Free Laws: Bismarck, Dickinson, Walhalla, and Williston.

Ohio

Definition: 1. *Alternative nicotine product means... an electronic cigarette or any other product or device that consists of or contains nicotine that can be ingested into the body by any means, including, but not limited to, chewing, smoking, absorbing, dissolving, or inhaling."*

2. Electronic cigarette means...any electronic product or device that produces a vapor that delivers nicotine or any other substance to the person inhaling from the device to simulate smoking and that is likely to be offered to or purchased by consumers as an electronic cigarette, electronic cigar, electronic cigarillo, or electronic pipe."

State Laws: 1. *Alternative nicotine products must be sold in the same minimum quantities as manufacturer's container.*

2. Sale/distribution of alternative nicotine products to persons under age 18 prohibited.

3. *Internet sales/distribution of alternative nicotine products restricted to transactions using age verification.*

4. *Vending machine sales restricted to locations inaccessible to persons under age 18 or where control of the vending machine is in the hands of the owner and is withinthat person's or other employees' plain view.*

State Smoke Free Laws: None

Cities that include vaporizers in their Smoke Free Laws: Bexley and Oberlin.

Oklahoma

Definition: 1. *Vapor product means "noncombustible products, that may or may not contain nicotine, that employ a mechanical heating element, battery, electronic circuit, or other mechanism, regardless of shape or size, that can be used to produce a vapor in a solution or other form. 'Vapor products' shall include any vapor cartridge or other container with or without nicotine or other form that is intended to be used with an electronic cigarette, electronic cigar, electronic cigarillo, electronic pipe, or similar product or device and any vapor cartridge or other container of a solution, that may or may not contain nicotine, that is intended to be used with or in an electronic cigarette, electronic cigar, electronic cigarillo or electronic device..."*

State Laws: 1. *Purchase/possession of vapor products by persons under age 18 prohibited.*

2. *Sale/distribution of vapor products to persons under age 18 prohibited.*

3. *Vending machines sales are restricted to locations inaccessible to persons under age 18.*

4. *Distribution of free vapor products to persons under 18 or on any public street, sidewalk, or park that is within 300 feet of any playground, school, or other facility used primarily by persons under the age of 18 prohibited.*

5. *Self-service displays of vapor products restricted to adult-only facilities.*
State Smoke Free Laws: None
Cities that include vaporizers in their Smoke Free Laws: None

Oregon
Definition: None
State Laws: None
State Smoke Free Laws: None
Cities that include vaporizers in their Smoke Free Laws: Benton County, Corvallis, and Cottage Grove.

Pennsylvania
Definition: None
State Laws: None
State Smoke Free Laws: None
Cities that include vaporizers in their Smoke Free Laws: Philadelphia

Rhode Island
Definition: *Electronic nicotine-delivery system means "an electronic device that may be used to simulate smoking in the delivery of nicotine or other substance to a person inhaling from the device, and includes, but is not limited to, an electronic cigarette, electronic cigar, electronic cigarillo, electronic pipe, or electronic hookah and any related device and any cartridge or other component of such device."*

State Laws: 1. *Electronic nicotine delivery system must be sold in original factory- wrapped package.*

2. *Retailers of electronic nicotine- delivery system products must obtain a license.*

3. *Sale/distribution of electronic nicotine delivery system to persons under age 18 prohibited.*

4. *Vending machine restricted to locked machines in locations continually supervised and in direct line of sight of authorized person on a business premises or in locations inaccessible to persons under age 21.*

5. *Distribution of free electronic nicotine-delivery system to persons under age 18 or within 500 feet of any school prohibited.*

State Smoke Free Laws: None

Cities that include vaporizers in their Smoke Free Laws: None

South Carolina

Definition: 1. *Alternative nicotine product means "a product, including electronic cigarettes, that consists of or contains nicotine that can be ingested into the body by chewing, smoking, absorbing, dissolving, inhaling, or by any other means."*

2. *Electronic cigarette means "an electronic product or device that produces a vapor that delivers nicotine or other substances to the person inhaling from the device to simulate smoking, and is likely to be offered to, or purchased by, consumers as an electronic cigarette, electronic cigar, electronic cigarillo, or electronic pipe."*

State Laws: 1. *Sale/distribution of alternative nicotine products to persons under age 18 years prohibited.*

2. *Purchase/possession of alternative nicotine products by persons under age 18 prohibited.*

3. *Vending machine sales restricted to locations inaccessible to persons under age 18 or locked and under control of owner*

State Smoke Free Laws: None

Cities that include vaporizers in their Smoke Free Laws: Denmrk, Estill, Hartsville, Inman, West Pelzer, and Yemassee.

South Dakota

Definition: *Vapor product means "any noncombustible product containing nicotine that employs a heating element, power source,* *electronic circuit, or other electronic, chemical, or mechanical means, regardless of shape or size, that can be used to produce vapor from nicotine in a solution or other form. The term, vapor product, includes any electronic cigarette, electronic cigar, electronic cigarillo, electronic pipe, or similar product or device and any vapor cartridge or other container of nicotine in a solution or other form that is intended to be used with or in an electronic cigarette, electronic cigar, electronic cigarillo, electronic pipe, or similar product or device."*

State Laws: 1. *Sale/distribution of vapor products to persons under age 18 prohibited.*

2. *Purchase/possession/ use of vapor products by persons under age 18 prohibited.*

3. *Distribution of free vapor products within 500 feet of playground, school or other child-focused facility prohibited.*

4. *Self-service displays of vapor products restricted to tobacco specialty store or vending machines inaccessible to persons under age 18.*

State Smoke Free Laws: None

Cities that include vaporizers in their Smoke Free Laws: None

<u>Tennessee</u>

Definition: *Vapor Product means "[(A)]any noncombustible product containing nicotine or any other substance that employs a mechanical heating element, battery, electronic circuit, or other mechanism, regardless of shape or size, that can be used to produce or emit vapor; (B) Includes any electronic cigarette, electronic cigar, electronic cigarillo, electronic pipe, or similar product, and any vapor cartridge or other container of a solution containing nicotine or any other substance that is intended to be used with or in an electronic cigarette, electronic cigar, electronic cigarillo, electronic pipe, or similar product..."*

State Laws: 1. *Liquid nicotine must be sold in child-resistant*

packaging, except pre- filled cartridges not intended to be opened by consumer.

2. *Sale/distribution of vapor products to persons under age 18 years prohibited.*

3. *Purchase/possession of vapor products by persons under age 18 prohibited.*

State Smoke Free Laws: None

Cities that include vaporizers in their Smoke Free Laws: None

Texas

Definition: None

State Laws: None

State Smoke Free Laws: None

Cities that include vaporizers in their Smoke Free Laws: Bedford, Boerne, Bonham, Burkburnett, Denton, El Paso, Frisco, Georgetown, Harlingen, Highland Village, Joshua, Lufkin, San Angelo, San Marcos, Sherman, Socorro, Waxahachie, Weatherford, and Wichita Falls.

Utah

Definition: 1. *Electronic cigarette means "(i) an electronic device used to deliver or capable of delivering vapor containing nicotine into a person's respiratory system; or (ii) any component of or accessory intended for use with the device described in subsection [(i)]; or (iii) an accessory sold in the same package as the device described in subsection [(i)]. (b) "Electronic cigarette" includes an e-cigarette as defined in §26- 38-2."*

2. *E-cigarette means "[(a)] any electronic oral device: (i) that provides a vapor of nicotine or other substance; and (ii) which simulates smoking through its use or through inhalation of the device; and (b) includes an oral device that is: (i) composed of a heating element, battery, or electronic circuit; and (ii) marketed,*

manufactured, distributed, or sold as: (A) an e-cigarette; (B) e-cigar; (C) e-pipe; or (D) any other product name or descriptor, if the function of the product meets the definition of subsection [(a)]."

3. Electronic cigarette product means "an electronic cigarette or an electronic cigarette substance."

4. Electronic cigarette substance means "any substance, including liquid containing nicotine, used or intended for use in an electronic cigarette."

State Laws: *1. Department of Health directed to establish rules for labeling, packaging and quality controls for electronic cigarette substances, except those sold in manufacturer- sealed container not intended to be opened by consumers, to be implemented by July 1, 2016.*

2. Selling/distributing electronic cigarettes to persons under age 19 prohibited.

3. Purchase/ possession of electronic cigarette by person aged 18 years prohibited.

4. Self-service displays and vending machine sales restricted to locations inaccessible to persons under age 19 without a parent or guardian.

5. Tobacco retail specialty businesses (tobacco product sales, including e-cigarettes, account for more than 35% of total annual gross receipts) must be licensed by counties and municipalities.

6. Location of tobacco retail specialty businesses minimally restricted relative to schools, child care facilities, churches, libraries, playgrounds, other tobacco specialty shops, and other facilities.

7. Retailers of electronic cigarette products must obtain a license from the State Tax Commission.

State Smoke Free Laws: *1. Electronic cigarettes prohibited in correctional facilities.*

2. School boards directed to adopt rules prohibiting use and possession of electronic cigarettes on school property and at sponsored activities.

Cities that include vaporizers in their Smoke Free Laws: Davis County

Vermont

Definition: *Tobacco substitute means "products, including electronic cigarettes or other electronic or battery- powered devices, that contain and are designed to deliver nicotine or other substances into the body through inhaling vapor..."*

State Laws: *1. Liquid nicotine must be sold in child-resistant packaging, excluding pre- filled cartridges not intended to be opened by consumer.*

2. Sale/distribution of tobacco substitutes to persons under age 18 prohibited.

3. Purchase/possession of tobacco substitutes by persons under age 18 prohibited.

4. Retailers of tobacco substitutes required to obtain a license.

5. Self-service displays restricted to locations inaccessible to minors.

State Smoke Free Laws: *1. Use of tobacco substitutes prohibited at child care facilities.*

2. Use of tobacco substitutes prohibited on public school grounds and at sponsored events.

Cities that include vaporizers in their Smoke Free Laws: None

Virginia

Definition: *Nicotine vapor product means "any noncombustible product containing nicotine that employs a heating element, power source, electronic circuit, or other electronic, chemical, or mechanical means, regardless of shape or size, that can be used to produce vapor from nicotine in a solution or other form. 'Nicotine vapor product' includes any electronic cigarette, electronic cigar, electronic cigarillo, electronic pipe, or similar product or device and* *any cartridge or other container of nicotine in a solution or other form that is intended to be used with or in an electronic cigarette, electronic cigar, electronic cigarillo, electronic pipe, or similar product or device."*

State Laws: 1. *Liquid nicotine must be sold in a child-resistant container and must include a warning label stating that the container should be kept out o the reach of children.*

2. *Sale/distribution of nicotine vapor products to persons under age 18 prohibited.*

3. *Purchase/possession of nicotine vapor product by person under age 18 prohibited.*

State Smoke Free Laws: *School boards directed to develop and implement policy to prohibit e- cigarette use on school bus, school property and at school-sponsored activities.*

Cities that include vaporizers in their Smoke Free Laws: None

Washington

Definition: *Vapor product means "a noncombustible tobacco-derived product containing nicotine that employees a mechanical heating element, battery, or circuit, regardless of shape or size, that can be used to heat a liquid nicotine solution contained in cartridges...."*

State Laws: *Sale of vapor products to persons under age 18 prohibited.*

State Smoke Free Laws: *Use of electronic cigarettes on public institutions of higher education restricted through regulation. (e.g., Eastern Washington University)*

Cities that include vaporizers in their Smoke Free Laws: Grant County, King County, and Pasco.

West Virginia

Definition: 1. *Tobacco Product and Tobacco-Derived Product means "any product, containing, made or derived from*

tobacco, or containing nicotine derived from tobacco, that is intended for human consumption, whether smoked, breathed, chewed, absorbed, dissolved, inhaled, vaporized, snorted, sniffed or ingested by any other means, including but not limited to cigarettes, cigars, cigarillos, little cigars, pipe tobacco, snuff, snus, chewing tobacco or other common tobacco- containing products. A 'tobacco-derived product' includes electronic cigarettes or similar devices, alternative nicotine products and vapor products..."

2. Vapor Product means "any non-combustible product containing nicotine that employs a heating element, power source, electronic circuit or other electronic, chemical or mechanical means, regardless of shape and size, that can be used to produce vapor from nicotine in a solution or other form. 'Vapor Product' includes any electronic cigarette, electronic cigar, electronic cigarillo, electronic pipe or similar product or device, and any vapor cartridge or other container of nicotine in a solution or other form that is intended to be used with or in an electronic cigarette, electronic cigar, electronic cigarillo, electronic pipe or similar product or device. ..."

State Laws: *1. Sale/distribution of vapor products to persons under age 18 years prohibited.*

2. Vending machine sales of vapor products restricted to adult-only establishments or establishments with an alcoholic beverage license.

3. Possession of tobacco products or tobacco-derived products by persons under age 18 prohibited.

State Smoke Free Laws: *Use of tobacco- derived products prohibited in schools and on school grounds except those areas not used for instructional purposes and inaccessible to students.*

Cities that include vaporizers in their Smoke Free Laws: Barbour County, Berkeley County, Brooke County, Calhoun County, Grant County, Greenbrier County, Hancock County, Lewis County, Marshall County, Mineral County, Monroe County, Morgan

County, Nicholas County, Pleasants County, Randolph County, Ritchie County, Roane County, Taylor County, Upshur County, Webster County, Wirt County, Wood County, and Wyoming County.

Wisconsin
Definition: *Nicotine Product means "a product that contains nicotine and is not any of the following: (1) a tobacco product; [or] (2) a cigarette."*

State Laws: 1. *Sale/distribution of nicotine products to persons under age 18 prohibited.*

2. *Purchase/possession of nicotine products by persons under age 18 prohibited.*

State Smoke Free Laws: None

Cities that include vaporizers in their Smoke Free Laws: None

Wyoming
Definition: 1. *Tobacco Products means "any substance containing tobacco leaf, or any product made or derived from tobacco that contains nicotine, including, but not limited to, cigarettes, electronic cigarettes, cigars, pipe tobacco, snuff, chewing tobacco or dipping tobacco."*

2. *Electronic Cigarette means "a product that employs any mechanical heating element, battery or electronic circuit, regardless of shape or size, that can be used to deliver doses of nicotine vapor by means of heating a liquid nicotine solution contained in a cartridge or other delivery system."*

State Laws: 1. *Liquid nicotine containers sold to in-state consumers must be in child-resistant packaging.*

2. *Sales/distribution /delivery of tobacco products to persons under age 18 prohibited.*

3. *Purchase of tobacco products by persons under age 18 prohibited.*

4. *Possession/use of tobacco products by persons under age 18 prohibited.*

5. *Self service displays restricted to vending machines in locations inaccessible to persons under age 18.*

State Smoke Free Laws: None

Cities that include vaporizers in their Smoke Free Laws: None

So the conclusion to all this is simple. If you want to vape on your vacation and not have to worry about local or state laws; you have three choices. Take your vacation in either Maine or Nevada. But then… you also could take it in Washington D.C. The federal lawmakers aren't stupid. Even they do not want to be regulated when it comes to vaping.

Ripping Clouds: The Truth About Vaping

Kimo Kiyabu

WIRE...COTTON..TOXINS...OH MY

"Those vaporizers are worst than cigarettes! Your smoking formaldehyde!" I have heard so many statements like this over the years that I have been vaping. When the powers that be can not find problems with the eLiquid then they try to go after the unit itself. They break it down, analyzing every part, and try to find a way to say that the vaporizer is worse than cigarettes.

In this chapter I will break down the vaporizer in order to separate fact from myth. I will go over the internal parts of the vaporizer starting with the Atomizer.

The Atomizer is responsible for creating the vapor by charging coils that heat up cotton soaked with eLiquid. Inside the Atomizer you will see one or two coils made of metal wire. Threaded through the middle of the coils is organic cotton. The first item I'll go over is the types of wire that is used to create the coils that look similar to spring coils.

There are four types of wire that is used, however, only two of those four are predominately used. The first of which is called Kanthal.

Kanthal is a brand of wire that is made from iron, chromium, and aluminum. It can resist temperatures up to 2,730° Fahrenheit. When heated it creates an excellent, non-scaling surface oxide, that protects from releasing toxins. It is important to remember that on average; a vaporizer heats up to a temperature of 572° Fahrenheit. Some statements concerning the metal wires are obvious fabrications like wire coils liquifying inside the atomizer. Kanthal is one of two wires that is recommended for use with a vaporizer.

The other recommended wire is Nichrome. This is an alloy made from 80% nickel and 20% chromium. Similar to Kanthal, when heated Nichrome creates a protective layer of chromium oxide. Both Kanthal and Nichrome are used in household appliances as the heating element because of the protective layer they create when heated. Nichrome, which was invented in 1905, can be heated up to a temperature of 2,550° Fahrenheit. There has been no scientific research stating that either wire is hazardous to the user when used with a vaporizer.

The two metals not recommended for use with the vaporizer is Titanium and pure Nickel. These wires have not been proven and can pose serious harm. There have been many reports concerning Titanium wires combusting into flame. And could be the cause of many biased research reports stating that formaldehyde had been detected in the vapor. Nickel on the other hand, has been known to cause problems for those who are allergic to nickel. Approximately 10-20% of Americans are allergic to nickel.

Formaldehyde is found in the combustion or burning of methane. For instance in forest fires or cigarette smoke.

But one must remember that there is no combustion in a vaporizer. It is simply heating a liquid to the point of vapor. So therefore the only way to create formaldehyde in a vaporizer, is to put dry cotton in the coil, and trigger the coils. The heat from the coils will then cause the dry cotton to combust. But then...that is no longer a vaporizer. It's a torch.

For the most part, all the users of vaporizers that I have seen, have common sense. Your not likely to find a user that will let the cotton of the vaporizer dry out and then continue to vape.

Since we are on the subject of cotton, let's talk about the different types. It is recommended by vapors worldwide to use some form of organic cotton. Like with anything else organic, the reason has to do with pesticides. Organic cotton is made from non genetically modified plants, non synthetic agricultural chemicals such as fertilizers or pesticides.

In recent years Japan has started multiple cotton projects to help revitalize the agriculture industry in Japan. Soon vapor users began using 100% Japanese organic cotton. Japanese cotton differs from other cottons in that it has shorter fibers. Making it a much denser product. When manufactured for vaping, it is formed into sheets, making it easier to work with; when building Atomizers. The density in turn allows for better absorption of eLiquid. Many users feel the vapor that comes from using the Japanese cotton is very taste forward and very clean as well.

There has been no scientific research at all stating that there is any toxins whatsoever in the Japanese cotton. This cotton has become the norm with vapor users. Still yet, another report stated vaporizers create Acrolein. Again Acrolein is only created when cotton is burned from combustion. Causing much doubt to the validity of the report. As hard as they try Big Pharm, Big Tobacco, and lawmakers still can not ignore the fact that science has actually only said one thing. Vaporizers are nothing except beneficial to ones health.

WHAT I WISH I KNEW BUT DIDN'T...THE HOW TO QUIT SMOKING CHAPTER

I stood on my front porch, took a long drag of my cigarette, and exhaled as I shook my ass off. It was December 20, 2012 and the temperature was thirty-one degrees. That would be my last day of sucking smoke. If your not motivated to quit the cancer sticks, don't try. You will fail. The fact that my testicles shrunk to raisins every time I wanted a cigarette and my doctor had told me earlier that day my high blood pressure was due to my smoking—was all the motivation I needed for me to quit.

The next day I had been eager to jump on the vape train. I went to my computer, search the internet at ten in the morning, found a vapor store close to my home, and made a bee line with wallet in hand.

At the time the only type of vaporizers for purchase had been the Joye eGo. They were about the size of a Sharpie marker. The battery would screw into a slim tank atomizer. The atomizer itself would have to be thrown away every two to three weeks and replaced with a new one. Each atomizer would cost around a dollar.

The particular kit that I had bought cost a hundred dollars. It included two batteries, one that would last around four hours, and was around two inches in length. The other lasted around eight hours and had been four inches in length. The kit also included two atomizers and a USB battery charger.

Many people bought these units when they tried to quit smoking. The problem with this type of vaporizer had been the hit of the vaporizer was not proportionate to that of a cigarette. So many people gave up after purchasing this unit and went back to cigarettes. I on the other hand had been determined and started researching.

I came across a different atomizer called the iClear 30. This atomizer could hold three milliliters of e-liquid versus the one milliliter the eGo atomizer held. But the biggest difference had been the heating coil in the tank itself. The coil was replaceable and five coils cost fifteen dollars. What I loved about the coil—the hit was very close to that of a cigarette. This tank helped me to stay off the cigarettes and continue with vaping. The only downfall was that the eGo batteries life would be cut in half because of the coil.

The iClear 30 was a product of a company called Innokin. Since their tank worked so well I decided to look at what type of batteries they had. That's when I first found out about Mods. Mods are steel tubes that hold the battery for a vaporizer. They got their name from the word *modification*. Back in the cave man days of eLiquid vaporizers, people used to convert, or modify flashlights into vaporizers. I purchased their Mod called iTaste 134. The iTaste 134 put me in vape heaven. This Mod allow me to adjust the wattage increasing the power to the atomizer. Enabling a draw that equaled a cigarette. When I began vaping with the eGo, my eLiquid was at eighteen milligrams of nicotine. When I started using the Mod I had to drop down to twelve milligrams of nicotine. I probably would have been happy with this set up if I had not lost it during the roller coaster ride Space Mountain.

I learned that day to always have a back up Mod. For the next two days I had to go back to the electronic cigarettes. That was like living in a mansion for years then having to go back to living in a halfway house. Absolutely disgusting.

So I had to buy a new set up and I wanted to get a bigger hit. I moved up to my first Rebuildable Tank Atomizer. I was excited as I purchased the wire, the wick and the tank. When you first purchase a rebuildable unit the vapor shop will put your first build on it. After the build and the tank had been filled, I took a drag, all I could think was, "wow—this is better than a cigarette." But after the third drag I knew I needed to go down to six milligrams of nicotine. The mod I was using was a Mechanical Mod. My first as well, but I would soon see the problems.

The Mechanical Mod I had purchased had a trigger that stuck out from the bottom. Between the base of the Mod and the trigger was a washer type ring. It could be adjusted to lock the trigger and keep it from firing in your pocket. I would always have trouble with the locking ring getting stuck, then the trigger assembly would loosen all the time, causing the trigger to fall out.

This entire set up gave me problems from the get go. When I tried to build the atomizer for the first time it took me two hours. Trying to create the coils, trying to connect the coils to the posts, it was such a hassle. I eventually became tired of dealing with all the problems and decided it was time for a new set up.

The next set up I bought was a digital Mod that the user could adjust both voltage and wattage. On top of that it had a built in ohm meter. It was simple to use and I bought an updated version of the i30 atomizer called the i30s.

But to my surprise, the i30s just wasn't cutting it after I had vaped on the rebuildable atomizer. I had ruined myself for the pre-built coil tanks. I tried different types of tank atomizers with coils that didn't have to be built. The Kanger Tech Pro Tank, the Nautilus by Aspire that even had adjustable airflow. But they were all big disappointments. I knew I had to figure out how to build my own coils.

One day I decided I would buy a full blown Rebuildable atomizer without the tank. The shop owner showed me an atomizer called the Tugboat. The atomizer had only three posts and the holes to thread the coil wires through were spacious. I got the hang of wrapping the basic coil and found the Tugboat fairly easy to build. The draw on the Tugboat compared to the tank atomizers was amazing. Once again I had hit vape heaven.

Over the past three years that I have been vaping I have spent nearly a thousand dollars on equipment and supplies. So if your a current smoker and you are considering switching to a vaporizer, I am going to save you that grand.

Here's exactly what you should buy, first the Mod. Buy the iStick 100w by Eleaf ($40). I have used this digital Box

Mod for over six months and it works beautifully. I know some will disagree because the previous iStick 50 watt had a built in battery. You use to have to plug the Mod into a wall socket to charge. I will say this once. Never buy a Mod that you have to plug in to charge. Always buy Mods that use removable batteries. The iStick 100 watt is this type of Mod. Next the atomizer, buy the Hannya post-less by Blitz Enterprises ($35). This thing is incredibly easy to build. Sometimes when you buy atomizers with posts, the posts begin turning after a while. When they start turning, as your tightening the screws to fasten the coils, it can become a real problem. The Hannya has no posts, you just build the coils then drop them into the holes. Now how to build the coils. Well today even a first time builder can build a basic coil in seconds. To do this you want to buy the Kuro Koiler Tool ($12). Lastly you want to buy Kanthal wire, twenty-two gauge and one hundred percent organic Japanese cotton.

Any vape shop can assist you with obtaining all these items. This is the set up I have been using for six months and it's perfect for a person who wants to quit cigarettes and not miss smoking.

BLOW CLOUDS...NOT HOLES IN YOUR FACE!

This is not a joke. This is very serious. Simply put, this chapter may save your life. Recently there have been stories concerning Mechanical Mods blowing up while the user was vaping. In every incident the user had made a fatal mistake. The problem occurred in all cases when the user combined a Sub Ohm Rebuildable Tank Atomizer with a Hybrid Mechanical Mod.

Before we can understand how this happened, there is a few things that need to be explained. First let's go back to how the Atomizer is built. Inside there are two coils generally. The coils not only heat up the eLiquid, but more importantly they provide resistance. Resistance is measured in ohms. The second thing you need to know is how a battery blows up.

A battery explosion occurs when an abnormal connection between the positive and the negative occurs. When this happens there is no resistance or voltage drop across the circuit. This causes an excessive electric current back to the battery. High current through the battery's internal resistance causes heating which can generate gases, within the battery, causing the battery to burst. This is commonly known as a *short circuit*.

A Mechanical Mod is a "power on demand" system. Meaning there are no safety measures provided by a computer that prevents the battery from discharging or "turning on."

Finally, sub ohm vaping is when the coils, in the atomizer, provides less than one ohm of resistance. This is where the problem occurred. All three cases had a tank atomizer that allowed to be fired with less than one ohm of resistance. Not only was it a sub ohm atomizer but the atomizers connection was not adjustable. It had a spring action connection. When the atomizer had been connected to the Hybrid Mechanical Mod, an abnormal connection occurred, creating a short. When the user pushed the trigger the electrical current traveled in two directions. Part of the current traveled normal, as it should, to the coils. The other part traveled directly back to the battery through the abnormal connection, without any resistance, exceeding the safe amp draw limit, causing the battery to heat up and explode.

Whenever a user sub ohm vapes there is the risk that a battery explosion can occur. It is very common for the coils to fluctuate in resistance while a person is using their vaporizer. If the resistance on the coils is less than one ohm, there is no room for fluctuation. There are many things a user can do to protect themselves from the dangers of a battery exploding. First is understanding amp draw.

Most vaporizers use an 18650 size battery. Every battery has a *Continuous Discharge Current* and a *Maximum*

Discharge Current. In vaping you want a battery with a high Continuous Discharge Current. Now to figure out if your build is compatible with your battery you need to use this following equation. Volts your vaping at, divided by the resistance of your coils(in ohms), will give you how many amps your pushing. So Amps=Volts/Resistance. Lets say you have an MXJO 18650 3000mah battery. The continuous discharge current is 20 amps. So when your vaping you want to push 20 amps or less. Now lets say you like to vape at 65 watts or 3.8 volts. You built your coils and they read 0.23 on the ohm meter or on your digital box mod. So using the equation: 3.8 volts divided into 0.23 ohms of resistance equals 16.52 amps of continuous current. So these current MXJO batteries are perfect because you'll be pushing less than 20 amps.

The next tip would be to stop using a Mechanical Mod. Buy a digital mod that has first, a built in ohm meter. This way as soon as you tap the trigger you can see what ohm your coils are at. Second, the mod should have a minimum ohm requirement. Usually this will be at 1.5 ohms. So if your build is less than 1.5 ohms it will not fire. Instead the display will read *"low resistance."* Third, a battery meter. Usually a fully charged 18650 battery reads at 4.2 volts. Digital Mods that have battery meters will only let you drain your battery down to 3.4 or 3.3 volts. This is a safety feature that shuts the mod down because below 3.3 volts is no longer safe to pull from the battery and you risk blowing it up if you do so. Lastly, do not get a digital mod that you have to plug in to charge. Make sure the mod has removable batteries that you can charge in a digital battery charger. Mods should never have to plug in to be charged.

Also make sure your batteries are in good condition. The wrapper is intact. No physical damage. Make sure to buy a digital charger for the batteries. The digital charger should stop charging when the battery has reached its max charge. Over charging batteries may cause them to explode or catch fire. So one more time to make sure you understand this:

- Stop using Mechanical Mods
- Make builds 1.5 ohms or higher
- Buy a Digital Mod that has ohm meter, battery meter, and minimum ohm requirement of 1.5 ohms
- Use batteries with high Continuous Discharge Current
- Make sure your build amps do not exceed CDC by calculating $A=V/R$
- Make sure batteries are in good condition
- Do not overcharge batteries

Remember, whenever someone blows up their own face due to lack of vaping knowledge, that gives lawmakers one more reason to ban vaporizers.

3 YEARS LATER

It's been three years since I began vaping. The one question everyone asks, "is it worth it?"

I think back now to when I was still smoking. Paying forty-eight dollars for ten packs of cigarettes. Carrying body spray with me, wherever I went, to use after sneaking a smoke. Sneaking, yes I remember always trying to sneak away for a quick drag. Sneak here and sneaking there always worrying about getting caught at work for sneaking away to take a puff. Hearing my family always commenting how I smelled like a dirty ashtray. Having to roll all the windows in the car down to smoke, hoping my wife wouldn't smell it later. Remembering the black film that would collect on the inside of the windshield. Then having to roll all the windows up to smoke, when I visited my sister in California, due to their clean air act. I remember standing in the extreme cold or heat to puff on a stick. I remember quitting smoking for a week every year when I would come down with a chest cold.

Then I think about now. No more complaints about how I smelled. Being able to vape in the car, while my wife and child are in the car. No longer needing body spray to try to cover the smell of smoke. Being able to breath normally. Not having to take blood pressure medication; since quitting smoking caused my blood pressure to return to normal. Being able to watch television in my house and vape. The chest colds no longer a yearly occurrence just a past memory from when I used to smoke. Being able to breath normally, not sounding like a buffalo. When I smoked cigarettes I spent $175 a month in cigarettes. Now I spend a $120 a month in eLiquid. Yes, as I puff now in my home, typing this book, I can say it was the best decision in my life to start vaping.

The only thing that is upsetting now days is some of the vape shops that I walk into. For instance, I will ask for an item, like a spool of nichrome wire. Instead of just saying, "sorry were out of the nichrome right now." The clerk will say, "that's terrible wire to use. That stuff melts while your vaping. Then you inhale that stuff and get nickel poisoning. You should use Kanthal, we have every size in the good wire." They would rather lie and make up some reason why I shouldn't use the product. I think to myself, "I know they just want me to buy something, but they don't realize the damage they are causing. People in the industry should know what they are talking about."

As a vapor advocate, every negative comment, every negative news report, and every negative myth is very bothersome. As it should be to everyone who enjoys vaping. This industry has enough idiots spreading myth, rumor, and lies unsubstantiated by scientific research. We do not need industry professionals adding fuel to the fire, which could lead to business suicide.

The scientific data is there and has been there for

decades. Showing how the common vaporizer, that many of us grew up with during the cold season, has evolved. Allowing anyone to carry the preventive medical benefits with them. It is up to us, the vapor users, to become registered voters, and have our voices heard. This is a fairly new industry. An industry that creates jobs and financial growth. An industry that needs to be protected by its users. Yes, there will be accidents, as in the unfortunate Mod explosions in recent months. But I was relieved to see many industry professionals immediately using the resources available, videos, and photos. To investigate and determine what had caused the misfortunate incidents. Which brought up yet another good point. Whenever there is an airplane crash or other horrific incident, there are teams of investigators that go in to determine the cause. The world's policing agencies need to start assigning industry professionals to come in and investigate incidents whenever serious injury has occurred. Then when their investigation is completed and they have determined the cause of the incident. They need to announce to the world exactly what happened through media such as television and newspapers. Issuing warnings, removing products off the market, if necessary, to ensure it doesn't happen again. This did not occur with the recents explosions.

On July 14, 2014 it had been reported that a sub ohm tank atomizer made by, let's say, company X called the Snowflake atomizer, (again fake name). Caused a hybrid mechanical mod to explode, inflicting injury. But no investigation by qualified professionals had been done. There had been no announcement through major media sources. Then on March 10, 2015 it happened again.

Company X's Snowflake atomizer caused a hybrid mod to explode in California. Luckily the man escaped serious injury. Then it happened again, Company X's Snowflake atomizer caused a hybrid mod to explode in Florida. This time the man nearly died. Due to the lack of a Vapor Investigation Team that could have made an announcement. The following two explosions occurred, that could have been prevented. As well as the explosion that occurred in Colorado on November 23, 2015. In this explosion it was not Company X's Snowflake atomizer but a duplicate sub ohm tank atomizer made by a different company. The sub ohm tank atomizer, caused again, a hybrid mod to explode.

But since the lawmakers are more concerned with banning the vaporizer rather than making sure the industry is kept safe. There had been no investigation team assigned. There was no safety announcement made through major media stating a warning to those who had the sub ohm tank atomizer with a hybrid mod. Permitting the sub ohm tank atomizers and the hybrid mods to remain on the market. Essentially allowing the next three explosions to occur.

It's time for the lawmakers to quit trying to ban the vaporizer through Clean Air and Smoke Free acts. They need to embrace the vaporizer as a Clean Air alternative to smoking. And begin to work with industry professionals to ensure that vaping is kept safe.

I still have hope that one day people will stop ignoring the scientific research. That the world will embrace the vapor users. I say to you today, my fellow vapors, so even though we face the difficulties of today and tomorrow, I still have a dream. It is a dream deeply rooted in the

American dream.

I have a dream that one day this world will rise up and live out the true meaning of its creed: "We hold these truths to be self-evident: that all people are created equal."

I have a dream that one day on the steps of the Capitol the vapor users and the lawmakers will be able to sit down together at the table of brotherhood.

I have a dream that one day even the country of England, a country sweltering with the heat of injustice, sweltering with the heat of oppression, will be transformed into an oasis of freedom and justice.

I have a dream that my children will one day live in a nation where they will not be judged by how they live their life but by the content of their character.

I have a dream today.

I have a dream that one day, in California, with its vicious anti-vaporists, with its Senator having his lips dripping with the words of addiction and restriction; one day right there in California, vaporist will be able to join hands with non smokers as friends.

I have a dream today.

I have a dream that one day every state shall be free, every city and county shall be liberated, the smoke filled places will be made smoke free, and the non vapor places will be made vapor friendly, and the glory of the clouds shall be revealed, and all lawmakers shall see it together.

This is our hope. This is the faith that I advocate with. With this faith we will be able to carve out of the mountain of ignorance a stone of hope. With this faith we will be able to transform the disdain of our nation into a beautiful communion of brotherhood. With this faith we will be able to work together, to vape together, to struggle together, to stand up for freedom together, knowing that we will be free one day.

This will be the day when all of Earth's children will be able to sing with a new meaning, "My planet, 'tis of thee, sweet globe of liberty, of thee I sing. Land where my friends died, land of the human's pride, from every mountainside, let freedom ring."

And if America is to be a great nation this must become true. So let freedom ring from the restricted hilltops of New Hampshire. Let freedom ring from the confined mountains of New York. Let freedom ring from the controlled Alleghenies of Pennsylvania!

Let freedom ring from the deprived Rockies of Colorado!

Let freedom ring from the constrained clouds of California!

But not only that; let freedom ring from barred vapors of Georgia!

Let freedom ring from the enslaved people of Tennessee!

Let freedom ring from every man and woman of Mississippi. From every coffee shop, let freedom ring.

And when this happens, when we allow freedom to ring, when we let it ring from every vapor shop, from every state and every city, we will be able to speed up that day when all of Earth's children, men and women, vapors and non vapors, lawmakers and politicians, will be able to join hands and sing in the words of the people who just quit smoking cigarettes, "Free at last! free at last! thank God Almighty, we are free at last!"

REFERENCES

Harold Wilson Patent for the first electric vapor
https://www.google.com/patents/US1514682?dq=electric+vaporizer+patents&hl=en&sa=X&ved=0ahUKEwjk4veRvuXJAhWFLmMKHX26AjMQ6AEIXDAJ

Summary of a 3-Year Study of the Clinical Applications of the Disinfection of Air by Glycol Vapors.
Authors
HARRIS, T. N.; STOKES, J., Jr.
Journal
American Journal of Medical Sciences 1945, Feb Vol. 209 No. 2 pp. 152-6
http://www.cabdirect.org/abstracts/19452701859.html;jsessionid=ED1D4F518CB64544A179AB7FEA39DF06

Nielsen, S. S., Franklin, G. M., Longstreth, W. T., Swanson, P. D., & Checkoway, H. (2013,

September). Nicotine from edible Solanaceae and risk of Parkinson disease. Annals of Neurology, 74(3), 472-477.
http://www.nxtbook.com/nxtbooks/wiley/annalsofneurology_201309/index.php?startid=201#/200

Jasinska, Agnes J.; Zorick, Todd; Brody, Arthur L.; Stein, Elliot A. (September 2014). "Dual role of nicotine in addiction and cognition: A review of neuroimaging studies in humans". Neuropharmacology 84: 111–122. doi:10.1016/j.neuropharm.2013.02.015. PMC 3710300. PMID 23474015.

Heishman SJ, Kleykamp BA, Singleton EG (June 2010). "Meta-analysis of the acute effects of nicotine and smoking on human performance". Psychopharmacology (Berl). 210 (4): 453–69. doi: 10.1007/s00213-010-1848-1. PMC 3151730. PMID 20414766

VAPOR TERMINOLOGY

Adapter – Dual threaded device used to allow a specific style or atomizer, cartomizer, or clearomizer onto a different style battery. This allows vapers to have the vapor production of one style of atomizer, while using the battery life of another style battery. (example: connecting a 901 atomizer threading onto a 510 battery)

Advanced Personal Vaporizer (APV) – An APV usually consists of a bigger battery, and features things such as variable voltage or variable wattage. Also referred to as a modified e-cig (MOD).

AEMSA – This is the Association of American E-liquid Manufacturing Standards. It is an all-volunteer organization dedicated for creating safe and sustainable standards within the production process of e-liquids.

AFC – Air flow control

Airflow (adjustable airflow) – This is a part on most vaping tanks; clearomizers, atomizers, etc; that allows more air to be received in the process of vaping, allowing for more vapor, as well as cooler vaper.

All Day Vape – The e liquid that you personally enjoy

over any other and can vape on all day long without it getting old.

Allen key/wrench – A tool used to open mods or tighten screws in atomizers

Alternative Cigarettes – Another name for electronic cigarettes

American Wire Gauge (AWG) – This is the standard used in the United States to determine the resistance and diameter of the electric wire used to create the coils in atomizers.

Amperage (amps) – Amperage is the flow of energy along a circuit. In APV's the lower the amps, the less capable you are of using high voltages on low resistance atomizers. This is prevalent in high voltage upon low resistance atomizers in dual coil cartomizers or clearomizers.

Analog– It is a slang term used by the vaping community describing "traditional" cigarettes

Anodizing– A method used to seal and finish aluminium

Aqueous Glycerine (AG) – The process in which VG liquid is thinned with deionized water, making it less viscous.

Ass Juice – This is a common term used for rating an e liquid that tastes horrible. The main cause of this rating is by vapers experimenting with different e liquids and coming up with horrid results.

Atomizer (aka Atty) – The atomizer is contained in a metal housing that is screwed into the battery; and contains the heating coil, wick and mesh bridge. It is the component in a vaporizer that is responsible for heating the e liquid to the point of vaporization.

Automatic – A style of electronic cigarette battery that does not have a button to activate the heating element. They are unsealed which allows airflow. When the user draws on the mouthpiece, a special sensor within the atomizer is activated by changing air pressure.

Automatic Shutoff – A common safety feature found on personal vaporizers that only allows the discharge of a battery for a set period of time. The average shutoff time is 10 seconds, however it is usually a smaller amount of time in ecigs and disposables.

Battery (batt) – Commonly known as the most important part of a vaporizer, it provides powers the heating element that turns the e liquid into vapor. It comes in two different types: automatic and manual. Manual switched batteries have a button to activate rather than being activated upon inhalation. They range in sizes and most have an LED light at the end that lights up when it is activated.

BCC – stands for bottom coil clearomizer. The atomizer coil sits at the bottom of the clearomizer tank.

BDC – Another term for "Bottom dual coil clearomizer"

Blanks – Cartridges or cartomizers with dry filler material that is filled with e-liquid.

Boost – The circuitry of a regulated mod that allows it to fire above the applied voltage.

Box Mod – A box mod is any PV or APV that comes in a box shape, and comes in several different wattage selections. Some popular wattage classes for box mods are: 10-30 watts; 50-80 watts; 100+ watts.

BP -Shorthand for big pharmaceutical companies.

Breathing – the process of leaving an e-liquid open to the air so that any alcohol can evaporate off. Can mellow some flavors.

Bridge – A small metal wire U-shaped covering on the inside of an atomizer that is designed to wick the e liquid from the cartridge. It is coated in steel mesh.

BT – Slang for big tobacco companies.

Buck – The circuitry of a regulated mod that allows it to fire below the applied voltage.

BVC – Abbreviation for bottom vertical coils. A very popular design for atomizer coils.

Burner – slang for a traditional cigarette/cigar

Car Adapter – Device that you can connect to a USB charger and charge your e-cig battery in the car.

Cartridge (Cart) – A plastic or covered metal mouthpiece that is the third part of a 3-piece set and is usually stuffed with some sort of absorbent filler material that holds e liquid.

Cartomizer (Carto) – A cartomizer or carto is a combination of disposable cartridges and atomizers. The cartomizer tank is placed in the middle of the tube and is designed to hold to e liquid. It is typically made of poly-fill surrounding a type of gauze material that is wrapped around an atomizer coil and a plastic center tube for airflow.

Cartomizer punch (Carto Punch) – A device used for punching holes in cartomizers.

Cartomizer–Single Coil – A cartomizer that uses only 1 coil.

Cartomizer – Dual Coil – A dual coil cartomizer that uses 2 coils. Because of its' dual coil design, it is able to produce twice as much vapor.

CASAA – Consumer Advocacy for Smoke-Free Alternatives Association. It is a non profit organization that campaigns for the rights of e-cig users.

Cig-A-Like – Any PV that has the similar appearance of a traditional cigarette.

Charger – A battery charger used to recharge your e-cig battery once it dies.

Clapton Coil – A coil made with a large gauge of wire wrapped tightly by a smaller gauge of wire, like a guitar string.

Clearomizer – A clearomizer is a transparent version of a cartomizer, designed to let users know how much e liquid they have left. It is usuallly made of thin, and easy breakable plastic, to maintain transparency. Clearomizers hold 2-3ml of e liquid, depending on the size and design. It's two popular designs are Bottom Coil Clearomizer, and Top Coil Clearomizer.

Clouds – Due to the highly dense water content in vapor, The vapor that is exhaled when smoking electronic cigarettes is referred to as clouds.

Coil – The wire that is used to vaporize the e liquid by creating an electrical circuit. The coil is usually made up of Nichrome or Kanthal wire. In the United States, the wire being used to make it is measured in AWG, while the rest of the world measures in the metric system.

Coil Jig – A device that makes rebuilding your own coils so much simpler.

Coil Winder (Cheater Stick) – A tool used to wrap perfect coils every time.

Connection– This is the threaded piece that allows you to screw into an atomizer/cartomizer/clearomizer.

Custom Mod– Any PV or APV that was handmade from parts not designed for vaping. This can even include wooden Mods.

Cut-Off– A safety feature that automatically stops you from taking a drag on your e cig if you take a drag for too long. It prevents the atomizer from overheating. There are flashing LED lights that usually let you know the feature is being used.

DCT– Dual Coil Tank- A large 3 to 6ml Tank with a replaceable carto.

Debridge– Removing the bridge (and wick) from an atomizer.

Deck– The flat base area where the positive and negative posts sit on an RBA/RDA, which is designed to keep e liquid off of the battery connection.

Dewick– Removing the wick from an atomizer.

Digital Cigarette– Another name for Electronic Cigarette

Disposable E-Cigs– Electronic cigarettes that are designed to be used and then thrown away.

Doubler– A double-strength flavour, intended to be used in 50/50 mixes.

Dragon Coil – Can be either macro or micro coils, they are wrapped as normal but the wick is wrapped outside of the coil so that air can flow through the inner diameter. Can increase vapor production with enough air flow.

Draw– Vapers inhale from their mouth on the vaporizer mouthpiece.
Drip– To drip drops of e-liquid into an atomizer.
Drip Kit– A battery, atomizer chamber, and drip tip, designed specifically for dripping.
Drip On-Demand (DOD)– An add-on that is used to feed e liquid into your atomizer by squeezing the bottle. It makes dripping easier.

Dripping (DD; direct dripping)– Vaping by adding a few drops of e liquid directly into the atomizer chamber instead of using a cartridge. This is the method that gives the best vapor quantity and flavor quality.
Drip Shield– The drip shield is a round metal or plastic tube that slips over your atomizer. If leaking occurs on your atomizer, the liquid will leak into the drip shield instead of leaking onto your PV. It then returns the excess e liquid to the atomizer to be used.

Drip Tip– A mouthpiece accessory with an opening that allows drops of e liquid to be dripped directly to the atomizer/cartomizer without the removal of the tip.
Drip Well– A bowl shape on a mod where the female connector is located on the atomizer; that is designed to catch any e liquid that might leak out.
Dry Burn/Hit– Purposefully firing an atomizer on a battery without e liquid to saturate it, which results in the heating up, and glowing of the coil. This allows the cleaning of the coil by burning off impurities.
Dual-Coil Cartomizers – A new type of cartomizer that has two coils that provides the resistance instead of one.

E Cig Accessories– Additional pieces to enhance your experience using e-cigarettes. They include chargers, extra batteries, and things like cases and lanyards.

E Juice– The solution that is vaporized within the atomizer tank, comprised of Vegetable Glycerin, Propylene Glycol, and/or Nicotine and Flavoring. Also referred to as E-liquid, Juice, or Smoke Juice.

Electronic Cigarette Association (ECA)– An industry group formed in early 2009. It is made up of suppliers and manufacturers who combined resources to help keep the e-cigarette as a legal option for smokers in the USA.

Electronic Cigarette (e-cig)– An emerging alternative to traditional cigarettes that allows users to enjoy smoking without many of the harmful side effects. It contains e liquid that is vaporized upon inhalation and usually consists of flavors and nicotine.

Vapor Starter Kit–A Vapor Starter Kit is usually composed of 2 batteries, 1 or 2 cartomizers/atomizers/clearomizers and a mouth piece or drip tip.

E Liquid– Another popular name for e-juice.

E-NIC (Electronic Nicotine Inhaler) – another name for the electronic cigarette.

E Smoke – Another short/slang for Electronic Cigarette.

Filler Material (Abbreviated as Filler) – Material placed inside of a Cartridge that is absorbent. It is used to keep the liquid inside of the cartridge and regulate flow to the atomizer so no flooding occurs.

Flavor Cartridge– Another term for a cartridge, containing nicotine and flavors.

Flavors – This refers to the particular flavor of your e liquid.

Flooding – This occurs when too much e liquid is put into the atomizer. The indicator of flooding is a gurgling sound and the performance of the atomizer is sometimes negatively affected.

Fuse– A specially designed fuse for use in mechanical mods to prevent some types of battery failure.

Fused Clapton – A Clapton coil that has two or more wires in the core of it as opposed to one in a regular clapton coil.

Genesis Atomizer– An RBA that uses stainless steel mesh as a wick instead of the typical silica and sits on the top of a tank (usually glass) with one or more holes in the deck leading into the tank.

Glassomizer– A clearomizer that uses glass rather than plastic for the tank. Examples would be the Kanger Protank.

Goose Neck– A flexible extension for your PV. Goose necks come in assorted colors and sizes.

Grub Screw – A type of screw used in atomizer posts. The tip is pointed to better secure wires.

Heatsink – Heatsinks are fins or protrusions on a mod, atomizer, or drip tip designed to dissipate heat by allowing more airflow over more surface area.

Heat steeping – Heat steeping is the process of speeding up steeping by placing one's e-liquid container in a hot water bath or in a hot environment for any length of time.

High Resistance (HR)– An atomizer or cartomizer with a higher Ohm rating than the standard equipment. This allows you to apply higher voltage to the coil.

Hit– The inhalation of vapor.

Hot Spot– Areas of excess heat on the atomizer coil. Hot Spots are a known cause of Dry Hits.

HV– High Voltage /device that operates above the standard 3.7 volts.

HV Atty– An atty designed for higher voltage vaping, not for use with standard batteries due to low power.

HV Mod– A dual battery or boosted supply mod (modification) to allow higher power vaping.

Hybrid, Hybrid PV, Hybrid Mod– A combined topper and battery holder designed to fit together as one seamless unit.

ICR– Lithium Ion Cobalt Rechargeable Battery

IMR– Lithium Ion Manganese Rechargeable Battery

Inception Coil – A nano coil inside a macro coil made from one continuous piece of wire.

Joules – A unit of power used in temperature controlled mods. It is equal to the energy transferred (or work done) when applying a force of one newton through a distance of one metre (1 newton metre or N. m), or in passing an electric current of one ampere through a resistance of one ohm for one second.

Juice – Another name for e liquid.

Knuckle Head– An adjustable drip tip that can be set to any angle desired.

Kick/Kicked – 1. another way to describe throat hit 2. The PV add-on that allows you to put it between your battery and PV's spring and allows you to convert a standard Tube Mod PV into a Variable Wattage device

Kanthal Wire– Trademark for a family of iron-chromium-aluminium (FeCrAl) alloys used in high temperature applications.

Kanthal, Kanthal A1– Kanthal is a specific brand of resistance wire that is used in building coils for vaporizers, usually sold for rebuildables. Kanthal A1 is a specific grade of Kanthal wire which is widely known to be the best wire for coil use.

Leaking – E liquid can leak out of the bottom of the clearomizer/atomizer/cartomizer and onto the battery, which in some cases can cause damage to the device and causing a shortage.

LED– The end of most electronic cigarettes contains a light for a realistic effect and to alert the user when the battery needs recharging.

Liquid – Also referred to as e liquid, e juice, smoke juice, or just juice. This is the liquid that is vaporized when using a vaporizer.

Li-Po– The Lithium Polymer rechargeable battery; made of different material than the Li-Ion batteries.

Lithium Ion Batteries (Li-Ion)– Considered the strongest and most powerful batteries in the vaporizer market, coming in many different sizes and shapes.

Low Resistance (LR)– An atomizer or cartomizer with a lower Ohm rating than the standard equipment. This generally causes the heating element to get hotter faster and produces vapor more quickly.

Lung Hit-Alternative to mouth to lung hits, lung hits are inhales of vapor straight to the lungs. Usually requires massive airflow.

mA– 1/1000th of an amp. This number is most often used in reference to the output of chargers.

Macro Coil-Macro coils are 2.5mm in circumference

or larger.

mAh-Abbreviation for Milliampere-hour, which is used to describe the capacity or energy charge that a battery will hold before it needs to be recharged.

Manual– A vaporizer battery style that has a button that activates the heating element.

Manual Shut-off– A safety feature found on most manual devices that allows the user to turn off their battery with 5 clicks of the button in rapid succession in order to make it safe to transport.

Mechanical Mod (Mech Mod, Mech PV, Mech) – A vaporizer that doesn't have any electronics or wiring, it's just a metal tube with a mechanical switch that holds a battery and a connector for a topper of some sort.

Microcomputer– The smart chip that signals the battery to send a charge of power to the atomizer, effectively starting the vaporizer.

Microprocessor– The part of the e-cigarette battery that is responsible for controlling the heater and the indicator LED light.

mg strength -(Milligram strength per millilitre-(ml) - This relates to the percentage of nicotine contained within the e-liquid. For example, 8mg is 8mg of nicotine per ml = 0.8% nicotine

Micro coil– A Micro coil is 1.5mm to 2mm in circumference.

Miligrams (Abbreviated as mg) – The unit of measure for how much nicotine is in a cartridge. Typical levels include 0mg, 6mg, 8mg, 12mg, 16mg, 18mg, 24mg, 30mg, 36mg and 48mg.

Milliliters (mL)– The amount of liquid in a given container.

Mod– Short for modification. This originally referred to modifying a flashlight or a battery to be used in vaping, but is now commonly used to refer to any vaping device that is not a cigalike.

Mouthpiece– The end of the vaporizer the user puffs on, and places to their mouth. Some mouthpieces come as a drip tip or cartridge.

Mouth to lung hit – Vapor is pulled into the mouth first and then inhaled into the lungs. Can provide more flavor in the mouth.

MV (Multi-Voltage)– PVs that offer several different voltage settings predetermined by the manufacturer.

Nichrome Wire– The resistance wire used in atomizer coils. Patented in 1905, it is made from nickel, chromium, and (often) iron. A common ratio is 80% nickel to 20% chromium. Generally considered the inferior of the two commonly used atomizer coil materials in cartomizers/clearomizers/atomizers.

Nic Juice– Nicotine liquid; and it's also short for nicotine, the addictive substance in peppers, tomatoes, potatoes, eggplants, and tobacco.

Ni200/Nickel Wire – Wire that is pure nickel, it has very low resistance and is used with temperature controlled mods. Never use Ni200 with regular VW.

Nicotine (Nic)– The substance found within traditional and electronic cigarettes that creates a pleasant sensation. An alkaloid found in tobacco, peppers, tomatoes, potatoes, and eggplants.

Nicotine Level– The designated amount of nicotine per cartridge. The nicotine level is the amount of nicotine present in a cartridge or bottle of e-liquid. It is usually measured in mg/ml.

Nicotine Liquid– The nicotine solution that is vaporized in the e-cigarette. The liquid is contained in the cartridge.

NiMH– Ni-MH(Nickel-Metal Hydride)- Nickel-Metal Hydride batteries have no Cadmium added. and no memory effect so it can be charged or topped-off at any time without affecting battery life.

Noob– A new vaper, due to a quick learning curve required to even start vaping, people are usually a real noob for only 1 week.

No Resistance Wire– Conductive wire that is used in RBAs to complete a circuit to the atomizer coil. This wire does NOT heat up.

NRT – Common acronym for Nicotine Replacement Therapy

Ohm (Ω)-The standard unit of electrical resistance. A lower number indicates lower resistance and therefore faster heating.

Organic Cotton Coils- A new coil setup made by Kangertech. It features a larger heating section, with the addition of the Japanese organic cotton that lasts longer than the majority of other, cheaper cotton coils.

Parallel – Batteries are wired into a mod parallel to each other, increasing battery life at the cost of voltage

Passthrough – A device that plugs directly into the USB port of a computer or charger and allows the user to vape without having to worry about battery life.

PCC -Common acronym for Personal (or portable) Charging Case. This allows an electronic cigarette battery to be stored in and charged from the PCC battery while away from other power sources.

Pen Style – One of many styles of vaporizers available, resembles a ball point pen.

Personal Charging Case (PCC)– A slim and compact case that is designed to hold and charge vaporizers.

Personal Vaporizer (Abbreviated as PV) – Another name for a vaporizer, much different than an e-cigarette.

Propylene Glycol (PG)– One of two main substances used in the making of e-cigarette liquids. Scientifically proven to kill airborne bacteria and reduces chances of respiratory infection when used in a vaporizer.

Pipe Style– The Pipe style vaporizer is also known as an E-Pipe.

Primer– Some companies use a VG based primer for preservation and shipping. The primer is used inside the atomizer and on the coil.

Protected (batteries) -The battery has a computer chip that protects the battery and breaks the circuit in the battery from completing if the voltage goes too high or too low, the current goes too high or the cell temperature rises too high.

Priming/Prime – The act of preparing a wick to vape, usually done by adding a few drops and soaking the wick in e-juice or taking a few pulls without heating the coil.

Puff– The motion the smoker uses on the e-cig to get a hit.

Pull– Also known as the draw, or hit. What the smoker does to get the vapor hit from the vaporizer.

Rebuildable Atomizer(RBA)– Rebuildable atomizers vary in design. Some have fabric wicks, while some use mesh and kanthal. Rebuildable atomizers are meant to save on cost and be readily fixable.
RDA-Rebuildable Dripping Atomizer.
Resistance– The measurement of ohms that allows you to calculate the right amount of voltage to apply to get the best wattage necessary. It comes in two common different variations; low and standard.
Resistance Wire– The wire that is used in an atomizer coil and heats up when an electrical current is applied. It is typically made from Nichrome or Kanthal.
Ribbon Kanthal, Ribbon Wire, Ribbon– A type of resistance "wire" used for building coils. Ribbon wire has a flat cross section rather than round, as with traditional wire.
RBA – Rebuildable atomizer
RDA – Rebuildable Dripping Atomizer
RDTA – Rebuildable Dripping Tank Atomizer
RTA – Rebuildable tank atomizer
Sensor– The part of the e-cigarette battery that detects when the user has taken a drag.
Series – Batteries are wired into a mod in series, increasing voltage at the cost of battery life.
Silica– Material used for building wicks. This is generally used to refer to braided silica cord. Silica has a very high melting point, so it can be cleaned with an open flame like a butane torch.
Smart Chip– A computer chip located within the e-cigarette battery that allows it to function.
Smoke Juice – Also referred to as E-Liquid, Liquid, Juice, or E-Juice. This is the liquid that is vaporized when

using a vaporizer.

Smokeless Cigarette – A term used to refer to an electronic cigarette. This term is used due to the fact that no actual smoke is inhaled while using an e-cig.

Squonk – Squonk box mods are mods that have a modified 510 connection where a bottle of juice is in the mod and can be squeezed (squonked) to push liquid into the cartomizer, rda, or tank from below.

Stacking– A risky practice of stacking batteries to create more power than one battery alone can achieve.

Standard Resistance– A standard resistance cartomizer is typically 3.0ohm. A standard resistance atomizer is 2.5ohm.

Starter Kit – A kit that typically includes everything needed to begin vaping. Most starter kits come with 1 or more atomizers, 1 or more batteries, a charger and 4 or 5 pre-filled cartridges.

Steeping– Allowing your e liquid to sit either open to the air, or in a sealed container. This is generally not necessary in e liquid that has a high ratio of PG to VG. It is more often necessary in high VG ratio juices.

Stick Style– Any electronic cigarette that resembles the style of a traditional cigarette.

Stovetop coil – Stovetop coils are coils built to resemble the heating elements on electric stoves. Massive surface area is possible, some claim they can produce insane amounts of vapor.

Subbing- See sub-ohm. Coil or coils with an ohm reading below one are used to create more vapor by offering higher coil temperatures.

Sub-Ohming- The practice by experienced vapers to increasing the current from your specific battery and by (using the principles of Ohms Law), reduce the ohms of the coils below one to achieve massive vaping clouds.

Syrupy – Some e-liquid are very sweet. Syrupy is often used to describe them.

Sweet Spot– The balance of several variables needed to achieve a satisfying vape. These variables are most commonly; voltage, wattage, resistance, and the flashpoint of the juice.

Tailpiping– Direct Dripping without a Drip Tip

Tank– A special type of cartridge that holds considerably more liquid than cartridges with filler. Usually used with a cartomizer and sometimes an atomizer.

Thermal Runaway– A very rare but serious occurrence. A chain reaction that results in the fire and bursting of a rechargeable lithium based battery. This happens from a couple different possibilities: overcharging, short circuiting, stacking batteries, physical damage to the battery and other PV malfunctions.

Throat Hit– The feeling a vapor smoker experiences when the vapor hits their throat. Most desire it to feel like a cigarette with a full, yet smooth hit. This is commonly felt with increased PG percentage in the e-liquid.

Tiger Coil – A coil wrapped with a strand of regular kanthal twisted with ribbon wire.

Titanium wire – Alternative to nichrome, nickel, and kanthal wires. Can provide a cleaner flavor but tends to be harder to work with than kanthal. Often bursts into flames during dry burns. Is excellent for use with temperature controlled devices.

Tobacco Harm Reduction (THR)– Policy or practice of providing less harmful nicotine-containing products.

Toot– Also known as Pull or to draw from your electronic cigarette.

Topping Off– Adding a few drops of e-liquid into a cartridge, cartomizer or tank.

Triple-Coil Cartomizer – A newer type of cartomizer that employs three coils providing about 1.6ohms of resistance. They vape strong, slightly more so than dual-coils, and come in several sizes.

Tube Mod– Any PV or APV that comes in a tube shape about the size of a small flashlight.

Unicorn bottle – E-liquid bottles that hold 15 ml or 30ml with an easy to use tip for dripping. Great for carrying liquid when traveling or out on the town as an alternative to the shorter, fatter bottles.

Unprotected Battery– Any lithium based battery that has no protection for the overcharging or other situations that can cause thermal runaway.

USB Charger– An e-cigarette battery charger that lets you charge by connecting the battery to your computer's USB port.

Vapegasm– The experience you get when you put on a new atomizer or cartomizer. That first taste you get from your favorite e liquid.

Vapehole – A vaper that shows little regard for anyone around them and vapes as obnoxiously as possible.

Vaper – The name given to the user of the vaporizer.

Vaper's Tongue – This is a common problem among many vapers when they vape too much of one flavor, and their taste buds become desensitized to the flavor.

Vape Safe (Fuse)– The Vape Safe Fuse is a tiny disc shaped fuse for use with PV's. The fuse is an added layer of safety in addition to a good quality battery.

Vape Whore– 1. Someone who is constantly vaping every breath of their day;
    2. Someone that only ever sign up for a site or community to try to win stuff. They never contribute, only hang out to soak up free things.

Vapor– The atomization of e liquid which results in a fog juice vapor which is commonly accepted to be exhaled as water vapor (steam). This is the main visible factor in vaping that simulates smoke, but is a much safer alternative.

Vaporizer– A vaporizer turns a liquid into a gas or a vapor.

Vapor Production– Typically associated with juices. Indicates how much vapor is produced using an average inhale of a vaporizer.

Vaping (vape)-The use of a vaporizer – similar to the term smoking when referring to an analog cigarette.

Vented Battery Cap– A simple hole or series of holes that allow for the battery to vent harmful gases in the case that your battery goes into thermal runaway.

Vent holes-Special holes made in the casing of high-end PVs or mods, to vent battery gases away from the face in case of battery explosion.

Venting a Battery – The process where a battery is taken beyond its specifications and gas is released from the battery.

Vertical coil – Instead of leaving coils horizontal, they are rotated 90 degrees. Often allow for better airflow in rebuildable dripping atomizers.

VG (Vegetable Glycerine)– A common ingredient found in e liquid. Sweet tasting and of low toxicity, it is thicker than Propylene Glycol and is usually used where thicker liquid or vapor is desired or where a PG sensitivity is present.

Voltage– The amount of kinetic energy which, for our purposes, when paired with resistance creates wattage.

VOOP – The action in which one vapes while defecating.

VV (Variable Voltage)– Any PV, APV, or Mod that allows the user control over the voltage output of their device. Generally recognized as superior to regular PVs that have a static voltage output that cannot be changed.

VV Mod– A variable voltage mod. Usually has a removable battery and boosted supply. You can change the voltage to find your vaping sweet spot.

VW (Variable Wattage)– Any PV, APV, or Mod that allows the user control over the wattage output of their device across the atomizer coil. This differentiates itself from a VV device because the voltage is calculated to arrive at the set wattage.

Watt (wattage)– The amount of raw heat that the atomizer coil uses to vaporize your e liquid.

Wick– Wicks are used to deliver e liquid to the coil in vaporizers. Most atomizers use a wicks that are most commonly made from silica cord. However, wicks can also be made from rolled up steel mesh, fiberglass, cotton, and sometimes ceramic materials.

Wicking– The process of osmosis where more concentrated fluid moves to an area of lesser concentration in an effort to find equilibrium.

Wire– Generally refers to resistance wire used in building coils for atomizers.

Woody (Wood Mod)– Any PV or APV that is

handmade and fitted inside a wooden tube or box.

Wrap – One revolution of a wire during the process of building coils. Wrap refers to the process of "wrapping" a wire around a tool, usually a drill bit or screwdriver.

Zemea USP-FCC Propanediol – An alternative to PG in producing e-liquid.

Made in the USA
Monee, IL
02 February 2023

26920218R00066